# To the Ends of the Earth

Other Titles in New London Librarium's
Catholic Series

His Hands on Earth:
Courage, Compassion, Charism, and the
Missionary Sisters of the Sacred Heart of Jesus

Love and Death in the Kingdom of Swaziland

Promised Land:
A Nun's Struggle against Landlessness, Lawlessness, Slavery,
Poverty, Corruption, Injustice,
and Environmental Devastation in Amazonia

Be Revolutionary: Some Thoughts from Pope Francis

To the Ends of the Earth

Memoir of a
Missionary Sister of the Sacred Heart of Jesus

Sister Maria Barbagallo, MSC

Translated from the Italian by
Glenn Alan Cheney and Michael L. Bates

New London Librarium

To the Ends of the Earth:
Memoir of a Missionary Sister of the Sacred Heart of Jesus
by Sister Maria Barbagallo, MSC

translated by
Glenn Alan Cheney and Michael L. Bates

Original title: *Fino agli estremi confini del mondo*

Front cover art: "Farolitos," by Colleen Hennessy

Copyright © 2017 Glenn Alan Cheney

Published by
New London Librarium
Hanover, CT 06350
NLLibrarium.com

All rights reserved. Reproduction of any part of this book in any medium is prohibited except with express permission of the publisher or author.

ISBNs:
Hardcover: 978-1-947074-00-2
Paperback: 978-0-9985436-6-6
eBook: 978-0-9985436-7-3

To Sister Barbara Staley, MSC,
for her love of the Missionary Sisters
and the history of the Cabrinian mission.

But seek ye first the kingdom of God, and his righteousness; and all these things shall be added unto you.

Matthew 6:33

Contents

Introduction	*11*
An Unexpected Choice	*19*
A Big Window on the World	*25*
In the Tunnel of God	*35*
Everything Is Mission	*43*
1968: University and Vatican II	*55*
First Intermission	*69*
Opting for the Poor or for Communism?	*75*
Earthquake in Guatemala	*79*
Revolution in Nicaragua	*87*
Sandinista Ideology and Evangelical Commitment	*103*
The Matiguás Mission—Successes and Failures	*115*
Second Intermission	*147*
A Sister Tired and Ill	*153*
The New Ways of the Religious Life	*161*
Loneliness and Hope	*175*
A Parenthetical Pause	*181*
Return to Missionary Life	*201*
Obligatory Passages	*223*
To Live on Mission, But…	*235*
Fifty Years of Religious Life	*247*
Acknowledgements	*255*

Introduction

Not long ago, nuns, especially the uncloistered ones we see busy out on the streets, were seen as good but rather faceless people, almost like servants, always willing to lend a hand for the good but not very attractive models for the girls of today. We believed them to be capable only of set phrases, of little metaphors, of put-on smiles, not very convincing; to us, they seemed relics of the past. Not like the cloistered nuns—we had always seen something grand and romantic in their withdrawal from the world. We could imagine them drawn up in grand emotional and spiritual tempests, amidst sacred music and abyssal silences.

Only with Mother Teresa of Calcutta, who knew how to become a mass media star, has the active religious woman become a modern personage, compatible with our culture. But in reality, we still know little about nuns. For example, we don't know that there are 680,000 Catholic religious women in the world, compared to 230,000 religious men; and that they are divided into an infinitude of religious institutions. Including male and female orders, there are today more than 2,500.

We know little because nuns don't usually write—especially those of active life, continually busy with works and travel, habituated to put all their energy into action. We know little above all because nuns have taken their vows of humility very seriously. This marvelous capacity to act and at the same time efface oneself as a subject becomes, however, a limitation in contemporary society, where the self-image that one projects counts so much. As a result, it happens that their path is not highly valued, nor their mission understood.

Sister Maria Barbagallo's autobiography is a response to these problems, as well as a pleasant read. At certain points, it becomes a real aventure story, especially in the middle chapters where she recounts her life as a missionary in Nicaragua before and during the Sandinista revolution. The external adventures are paralleled by an interesting internal spiritual journey, a story of the difficulties and the beauties that stem from her choice of a religious life, narrated with perspicuity and sincerity.

Sister Maria entered the Congregation of the Missionaries of the Sacred Heart (MSC), founded by St. Frances Cabrini, in 1958. The founder of her Institute had been canonized a few years earlier, in 1946. Certainly that must have helped to ignite curiosity about her work. Maria Barbagallo, in fact, knew little

Introduction

about nuns, but she was deeply impressed by a biography of the holy founder that she had read.

Beyond any doubt, it was an account of a singular woman: Francesca Cabrini was born, the last of eleven children, in 1850 in Sant' Angelo Lodigiano, a Lombard farming village, in a family of modest farmers, practicing Catholics. Paternally, she was related to the anticlerical political leader Agostino Depretis. Her mother, Stella Oldini, came from a family of Milanese entrepreneurs who founded the De Angelis pharmaceutical firm. From her family culture, Francesca obtained not only religious fervor and a spirit of initiative, but also a sincere love for the Italian nation. This was not common among Catholics of that era, because national unification had ended the Pope's secular rule of the central third of the country.

Her youthful formation was guided by her older Sister Rosa and the parish priest, don Dedé. After him, she never again had assigned spiritual advisors or confessors, a truly exceptional situation for a religious woman in that era. At the end of childhood, reading the annals of the Propaganda Fide aroused in her a missionary vocation, but her entry to the religious life met many obstacles. With a teaching degree, she tried to enter various religious institutions, but was turned away because of her uncertain health. She was, however accepted by the Bishop's invitation in the Casa della Providenza di Codogno, an institution for poor children founded in 1818. There, in 1877, she took her vows with the name Saveria Angelica

13

del Bambino Gesù. The institute, however, did not meet her expectations at all. Living within it, and for a time directing it as Superior, caused her trials and suffering. The impossibility of reforming the institute brought the bishop of Lodi, finally, to propose to her the foundation of a congregation of missionaries. Francesca immediately found a new headquarters in Codogno and moved there 10 November 1880 with seven companions. In the first years, the new institute concerned itself only with female education and assistance to orphans, but in a short time its sphere was enlarged to other foundations, all in Lombardy, until the opening of a house in Rome enabled the grant of papal authorization and opened the doors to mission work. Knowing her organizational abilities, the bishop of Piacenza, Giovanni Battista Scalabrini, invited her to found a center for assistance to Italian immigrants in New York.

The start date was set for March 1889. Twenty years later, Francesca had obtained American citizenship. Thus began the American adventure that brought her to erect in the three Americas more than 50 institutes, and to be proclaimed by Pius XII, in 1950, patroness of emigrants. In 1952 the American Commission for Italian Emigration named her "the most illustrious emigrant of the century."

The first encounter with New York was not easy, but her tenacity overcame the many obstacles. Francesca began an impressive series of supportive activities, at first educational and then medical, for immigrants.

Introduction

"The Italians here are treated like slaves" (she wrote in those first years). "One would have to repudiate patriotism not to feel oneself wounded."

Her aim was to facilitate the immigrants' entry into American society, making them good citizens, but without repudiating their religious and national origins. This agenda was successful, thanks to the capillary action of a great many schools scattered strategically across America, and supplanted the previous concept, to insert individuals into American society at the cost of forgetting their own origins and repudiating Catholic faith. In a short time, her missionary activity expanded to other regions of the United States, like Denver, Chicago, Seattle, and New Orleans, then to Central America—Nicaragua—and then to the southern continent, Brazil and Argentina, any place that had colonies of Italian emigrants.

Francesca found herself forced to extend her activity to hospitals as well. Her renowned capacity to administer and organize involved her in a tense operation to rescue the Italian hospital in New York, Columbus, which had gotten into rough waters. In a few years, Cabrini succeeded in transforming it into one of the more important medical institutions of New York. In this instance, as always, it was thanks to her entrepreneurial gifts and her legendary capacity to raise money ("She didn't ask. There were admirers of her work to help her" wrote the Italian consul's wife.) that she succeeded in realizing an undertaking that seemed impossible. A few years later there was a Columbus

To the Ends of the Earth

Hospital in Chicago, one in Denver, one in Seattle.

Despite her precarious health, she was untiring. She crossed the ocean 24 times. At her death, which came at the age of 67 in Chicago in 1917, she left 67 institutions in eight countries.

Her intense spirituality emerged above all in her work, in her continuous activity aimed at using good to oppose evil. Her prayer was in deeds, not words. Her life was marked by perpetual activity. She wrote, "With your grace, most beloved Jesus, I will run after you to the end of the race, forever, forever. Help me, Jesus, because I want to do it passionately and quickly."

Enemy of all sentimentalism and whining, she sought always to keep a cheerful face. "Do we feel bad? We smile all the same." She taught her Sisters to face great responsibilities without fear, not to lean on anyone.

This strong, modern woman, able to deal in the business world, to build great things, and to guide Sisters in the spiritual life with a firm hand, attracted Sister Maria Barbagallo into the world of travel and adventure, even within herself. The figure of the founder, in congregations of active life, had assumed great importance. In fact, it embodied a new model of religious life for women—a model not theorized but lived. One understands, therefore, how this model takes on great importance both in the choice to enter the Institute as a Sister and in the construction of a true religious life.

Introduction

It allowed her to continue, and sometimes even to widen, her embrace of the world. It also allowed her strong autonomy within the Church, an autonomy based on the economic solidity and global distribution of her institutions. In fact, this allowed her to escape the controls of local clergy by speaking directly to the pope.

The incredible momentum that Francesca Cabrini had given to her foundation assured it longlived economic prosperity.

This complex structure, however, faced the risk of organizational rigidity, that could lead to desiccation of the spirit of a founder who was distinguished by the dynamism and promptness with which she grasped the opportunities offered by history. In the sixties the Cabrini Institute had entered a crisis, and the innovative actions of Vatican II were deeply influential in determining its renewal. The experience of Mother Maria lies precisely in these decades of transformation, lived first as a simple Sister, then little by little assuming higher responsibility, and finally elected, for two consecutive terms, Superior General.

Through this narrative we relive the fundamental problems that have shaken the Catholic world of our time: the option for the poor, harshly tested in the political upheaval in South America; the crisis of vocations, including those of women, in Western societies; and the radical discussion of the meaning of the choice of religious life today.

But equally interesting are the inner discoveries, told

with a simplicity that is almost always lacking in the narrative style of the religious. In particular, Sister Maria returns to the theme of loneliness. "Understand above all," she writes, taking stock of her long experience in Central America, "that to live their vocation significantly, Sisters must daily accept their loneliness—not the absence of love that makes us miss friends, acquaintances, family members, and customs, but that deep, unbridgeable loneliness that no one can ever overcome. This fact, absolutely personal, always represented my vulnerable roots, all together the unattainable mystery that was myself."

Along this long narrative path, we follow a thread of extraordinary attention to the beauty of the world, to landscapes—an exceptional sense of beauty. And this attention, combined with its simple style, modest even when talking about issues of high and heroic actions, makes this book, in many ways, similar to Willa Cather's masterpiece, "Death Comes for the Archbishop." Maria Barbagallo's memoir, too, can be said to be a joyous book through the happiness that comes from knowing how to appreciate the forms of the world.

1

An Unexpected Choice

Rome was sunk in the sultriness of early afternoon, but the sky, clean and blue, lit the facade of the parish church, in front of which Rosa, Giulia, Paola and I met for an appointment. They were my closest friends in the Catholic Action group. We were not extraordinary girls. Indeed, our family situation was that of many girls at the time—simple, penniless, with some inclination toward the cultural and, even more, the spiritual.

But we belonged to a category of people that was about to disappear. Our meetings in the parish were so poorly attended that it was hard to organize programs for the very young. Those of our own age were married and gone. Small new groups were arising and entering in competition with ours. We already felt a bit out of the present time. We didn't follow the latest singers of the moment, and the young men who courted us seemed like shallow boys.

Our points of reference were gradually disappearing. Some of the Catholic Action leaders had gone into a desert or the cloister. We had also joined political struggles for the Christian Democrats, but at that time—1958—we did not share certain behavior and were strongly critical. We read the *Cronache Social [Social Chronicles]*, *Il Regno [The Kingdom]*, *La Traccia [The Way]* and the news from the Citadel of Assisi. We knew something about the integral humanism of Jacques Maritain and understood that new times were coming. But we were not well-educated enough to seriously discuss what was happening. We were interested in Christian spirituality, the real thing, the authentic thing, even if with a hint of idealism.

My friends arrived a bit late because one of them had locked her keys in the house. She went to another house to ask for help, but they weren't getting anywhere, so we all headed to her home in hopes of resolving the problem. It was solved a little recklessly when, a few hours later, we jumped from the balcony of my friend's apartment next door. Fortunately, the door to the balcony was open. Somewhere there must be our photo with the key in hand.

We went to the convent of the Fathers of the Sacred Heart, near the Via Gregorio VII. Padre Pomes was waiting for us. Since he was the steward of the house as well as our ecclesiastical adjutant (as priests in charge of the sections of Catholic Action were called then), he invited us into the kitchen to meet the Sisters and eat delicious fresh bread with salami, after which we left together in his minibus, to get the luggage.

Padre Pomes followed us for several years. He was a serene and practical man with a thick black beard, long hair, and a black cap that he always carried on his head. He accompanied us in meetings and patiently endured our constant interruptions during class, especially those on "morality." He accompanied us on trips, in film clubs, and even back home when we finished late in the evening. But he did not know us too well. When he preached at spiritual retreats, we were a little disappointed. We wished he would speak of mysticism and high contemplation. We were a bit exalted, while he understood that we needed to keep our feet on the ground if we really wanted to aspire to holiness.

At home there was only my older Sister, Marotta. She had returned by sea with her youngest child, Enrico, because he was not well. She grew nervous to see me coming. I knew why and didn't say anything. She was uneasy with me and sprayed nervousness from every pore. The child was only two years old, a love, and I adored him. He looked at me with a worried look, sensing that something was happening and that it involved especially me. But he could not, of course, understand more. My mother was in Sicily in our "paternal home" (so to speak), an inheritance that my Father had received from a maternal aunt after his Father (my grandFather), who could not stomach his marriage to my mother, "punished" him by leaving him no inheritance.

My other two Sisters and my brother were also on vacation. I had been around Italy to greet them. To my mother, however, I had not gone. She was uneasy with me. She favored me a little. Widowed, she had suffered to raise a family with five children. Fortunately, my older Sisters were already working and helped a lot, especially my oldest Sister. My mother was expecting that I would be the comforter of her old age. When she saw that I was engaged to a lawyer who was a professor and that I was starting down a path of journalism and literature, she began to worry. Unbeknownst to me, she did some investigating and convinced herself that her uncertainty was confirmed. He was an atheist in poor health, and besides, she did not like him. She did everything to thwart me. She read letters that he sent me and commented on their style, angering me and producing the opposite of the intended effect. Poor mother, she didn't have much success with her daughters. Something similar had also happened with my Sisters. Since her pressures were unsuccessful, she began to pray, to make novenas, and I don't know what other vows to God. The relationship broke up. Now my mother felt guilty toward me because the relationship was over, but the result was not what she had expected: the return to the womb, or an epilogue in accordance with her expectations. So, to keep things simple, I had decided not to go to see her.

An Unexpected Choice

There would be time later. Before saying good-bye, my brother, knowing my passion for race cars, said: "If you change your mind, I will give you the Ferrari." He had just bought one in installments. As children, he and I had often played as Formula One drivers. When I didn't say anything, he gave me a gold chain from around his neck. My Sisters had made some objections, but then, a bit sadly (especially Rita, who was about my age), they faced the facts.

So I tried to avoid a direct meeting with my older Sister and I retreated to my room. Everything was almost ready, but I stuffed the last things into my duffel bag. My friends and Padre Pomes were waiting for me downstairs.

I was certainly sorry to leave Maretta that way. We owed her a lot. After the death of my Father, she was at the core of the family. She loved us a lot, helped us to finish school, and cuddled with us. Even after her marriage she continued to look after us. She was highly educated, taught me (and still teaches me) to appreciate good books, good music, good movies, good fashion. But perhaps she also taught me not to be afraid of my ideas and my aspirations: for that reason, after having contested my choice a bit, she couldn't argue any more; but she did not agree.

I finished tidying up the room that I was about to leave behind. Enrico, my little nephew, was turned around under my feet. It was amazing how he sensed the situation! I carried the really heavy suitcase to the landing and then turned back to say good-bye to my Sister. All I said was, "I'm going." I got no answer, so I went out while the baby was whimpering, "Auntie, auntie, are you going away?" I said then that we would meet again, and he said: "But you come back soon?" My heart was breaking. Among other things, the elevator was not working. I had to drag the suitcases with great effort. My Sister was behind the boy, pulling him inside. Padre Pomes met me to get the suitcases, my friends, and the other things. He asked me how it had gone. I said, "So-so."

We crossed the whole center of Rome, which was beautiful and deserted. In the car we chatted and laughed a lot as I let my tears flow. Sometimes Father Pomes said, "Calm down, girls."

When we got to Via Aldrovandi, Padre Pomes parked the van and took the heaviest suitcases. I think at that time he was the only person among us who had a little lucidity. The big iron door opened. We entered a large hall, clean, bright and full of plants. Some little greetings, an emotional and hasty farewell to my friends, who had stopped laughing. Then a tall, kind nun offered us something to drink, but we all said no. I said goodbye to the Padre, and when the door closed behind us, I became aware that my life was changing completely. I had entered a convent.

2

A Big Window on the World

The big house that had welcomed me had, inside, a life all its own. Everyone worked, prayed, and studied, and everything was organized in rhythms, timetables, rules that worked perfectly, or so it seemed. Time was marked by a schedule to which they all adapted with no apparent problems. After a few days spent in a neutral area (a kind of antechamber of the religious Community), I was welcomed into the Community. I wore a long, black dress, but I didn't have the veil. When the Superior introduced me to the Sisters, I received smiles and encouragement. I didn't know much about the Congregation. I had only read about the life of the founder, St. Francesca Cabrini, and I was fascinated. When a Sister asked me how I came to know about the Congregation, I remembered the only significant episode.

A few years before, the delegate of the diocesan Catholic Action which dealt with the arts, had invited each of the sections of Rome to prepare a small play to be presented in a large assembly. The best work would be awarded a prize. I had a great passion for theater. I invented something of which I remember neither the title nor the plot, and I called on my "young girls" (as girls aged 12 to 16 were called) to be our delegates. From the whole Diocese three works were chosen to be presented right there at the Missionary Sisters of St. Frances Cabrini on Via Aldrovandi. Our section won, and they gave us an award. On that occasion, to set the scene, I made a fool of a Sister, and I admired her kindness. Then, the same day, when we came out of a heavy rain into the magnificent lobby, our umbrellas dripped all over the floor. Accustomed as I was to getting blamed for things, I was quick to apologize, but a gentle nun said, "Don't worry, we'll clean it up." This fact impressed me, and I asked the nun how one would enter the convent (which I'd already been thinking about for a while…). The nun had me talk to the Superior, who loaded me up with books about Mother Cabrini. Then, going into into the church, a beautiful chapel, I noticed above the altar the great fresco of Mother Cabrini with emigrants, and I prayed: "Mother, I do not know much of this Congregation, nor of you, but please take into consideration that I might be your Sister. " After that, I forgot what happened (or tried to forget). Events afterward did the rest.

A Big Window on the World

My vocation, however, was not born at that moment. In my family we practiced religion seriously, but the family was very critical, especially of priests and nuns. Papa was really an exceptional man for his faith and his constancy. He had been persecuted by the fascists for his liberal views, and perhaps the fact of his seeing so many of his friends and colleagues go over to fascism was what eventually crushed his fragile health. I remember that my mother got us the cards for a fascist youth group, "Little Italians," keeping it hidden from our Father, because if we didn't join, we wouldn't have rights at school. Papa was well educated. He wrote articles for newspapers (as long as he was free to write), poetry, and plays for the Salesian theater. He practiced his profession as a lawyer only for small fees; he was the director of a bank. He prayed a lot, and even during his long illness he always maintained a certain humor. He suffered from his Father's behavior toward him, from his friends who marginalized him, from the precarious condition of our family, and from the war. He died as the war was about to end.

Mother was a beautiful woman, authoritarian but very affectionate and witty. From Papa she obtained a taste for music and reading. She also prayed a lot.

But where I think I started a vocational journey, without knowing it, was in the parochial setting and as part of Catholic Action. As a child I attended the oratory and, later, Catholic Action. In particular I owe my introduction in spirituality to a mentor who had me read a lot of books about saints and spirituality: She had me comment and criticize. To her I owe so much. Her name was Angela Salemi. She was the one who had me read the biography of Mother Cabrini for the first time. It fascinated me to read about the lives of great saints such as Teresa of Avila, Elizabeth of the Trinity, St. Therese of the Child Jesus, St. Clare of Assisi, and many others. I liked also saints such as Francis of Assisi, John of the Cross, Francis Xavier, etc. I also read some medieval mystics, but while they touched me, I didn't understand much.

My life, however, was a mixture of secular and mystical aspirations. I liked to dance and have fun, to get noticed by young men, and I was very vain. At the same time, I liked to be alone for hours, looking at the sky and thinking about what might be beyond. I liked books and romantic movies. I empathized with the fate of so many desperate heroines dying of love. But I remained breathless before the figures of missionaries and martyrs, heroes and people who gave their lives for others. I do not know which genre matured more in the jumble of my heart. At the age of twenty, I said that I could not stand the nuns. At twenty-two, I said the same. At twenty-four, I entered the convent.

I did not have spiritual directors, at least in the classic sense. This was perhaps a great void and a great difficulty for me, but also an advantage. I had to always trust in God and in Him alone. And there is nothing more dramatic, but also nothing safer. I was not attracted by people, nuns, the habits, or the tranquility of the cloister. I can say, with some fear, that I was fascinated by God.

The early days were quite simple. I met many Sisters of great spiritual stature. At the time, there were about fifty in Rome. Though they showed certain limits—indeed some were particularly annoying— there was in them something great that hid under the austerity of their black habits. I remember a Chinese Sister, Mother Frances Tsen. She was very refined, a pianist who embroidered divinely and painted well. She led me into the garden to clean the flower beds, and she said, "Look how our soul should be—like a flowerbed cleaned well, but we need to keep it free from so many bad weeds, the small disordered tendencies that take away the fervor of our spirit."

Mother Alberta Oliveira, a Brazilian Sister, tall, elegant, an excellent pianist, was embroidering when she told me: "When I'm tired or bored, I think that each point of these stitches can have an infinite value if I do it with love and unite it with Jesus, for the missions, for the Kingdom of God."

Mother Cecilia Bottino was an intelligent, cultured and spirited Sister. She knew many languages that she studied on her own, even Russian.

Mother Alfonsina Seregni was the philosophy teacher. She listened patiently to my nonsense but then concluded: What matters is the true spirit.

Mother Attilia Forcato was a young Sister whose

transparency impressed everyone. She died very young and, we believe, a saint.

There were elderly Sisters who were a delight. Sister Nazarena Tirelli was more than ninety. She had such a fervor of spirit in everything she did that she left confusion in her wake. Sister Dionisia Locatelli was in charge of the refectory. They said she had been in the novitiate for many years because of her temper. She was ancient, lively, sly, critical, and with a good sense of humor. Some years later I was fortunate to assist her before she died. I asked her: "Sister Dionisia, can I do something for you?" She looked at me with her usual wit, then said to me, "Please go down and get me a glass of fresh water straight from the tap..." She had taken so many trips to the the Sisters' table, and it was terribly hot.

"Right," I said.

But as I was leaving she made a sign with her hand for me to come back. She said, "No, let it be. You know, these are the last chances that God gives us to deserve something. The devil is clever and likes to make us ruin ourselves." I obeyed her. Moments later, she died.

I remember many, the old and the young, the wise and the shrews, the cheerful and serious, of so many nationalities. There was something about them that conveyed the experience of God. Of Mother Edmonda Petrucci, the Superior, the Sisters said, "She is a lady!" And she really was.

It was not much trouble to pick up the rhythm of the day.

A Big Window on the World

I especially liked recreation. The Sisters gathered in a circle to work, some knitting, some crocheting, some painting, some embroidering or something for school. Mother Antonietta Echave, a Sister who had just arrived in the Community (later I learned that Sisters often switched communities), was Spanish and had been in prison during the Spanish Civil War. At recess she talked about the adventures she had lived through, but with a sense of humor that made us think we were watching a comedy. Every day during recreation we ran to hear the continuation of the story. She had fled from Spain in civilian clothes and had shown up at our House in Genoa. The Sisters would not let her in because they believed she was a lying vagrant. To be recognized she dropped to her knees to repeat all the prayers that were used in the Congregation. She was greeted with the tears of one and all.

After recess, in the evening, we went to church to pray the matutinal for the following day, then returned to Community where we discussed the meditation of the following day, generally on the Gospel, read an exhortation of Mother Cabrini, and then returned to church for the Compline evening prayers, after which strict silence began.

Prayer seemed laborious to me. Vocal prayers tired me; they were long and always the same. Also, sometimes the words of the prayers were so demanding that I was afraid to say them; for example: I want always to choose the worst—humiliation, suffering or anything like that. I understood the spirit of those words, but they seemed exaggerated. I liked the Divine Office, even if said in Latin. But I was not able to do a proper critique, even afraid to desecrate those things, and frankly I thought myself not up to that level of prayer.

The Sisters told me only the essentials. They would not tell me: "Do this" or "This is not done," I had to figure it out alone. I remember that for several weeks I thought I had missed dinner. In fact we had dinner at six in the afternoon. After dinner there were recreation, prayers etc., I thought that after everything was finished, there would be a real dinner, while the food we had at six o'clock seemed like a strange snack with soup! Along with everything else, I was also hungry. Then a Sister saw me turn away from the closed door of the refectory. Speaking very softly, she explained that those who had nothing to do were to go to bed. So, between one gaffe and another, I learned Community life.

In the background of the life passing before my slightly curious, slightly surprised eyes, was the wide world of missionaries. Everything directly or indirectly referred to the "mission": prayer, work, the chronicles of the Cabrini world mission that were read at the table, people coming and going, the packages that were sent off or those which arrived. I had no idea how vast this world was. My ears rang with the names of our missions: Denver, New York, California, Canada, New Orleans, Argentina, Brazil, Central America, Australia and then almost all of Europe. I only knew a little about Italy. I saw

A Big Window on the World

the Sisters fleetingly; they smiled at me, and rushed away. A great missionary exhibition at the entrance illustrated Mother Cabrini's travels, her foundations, the houses, her famous quotes: "Ardently and quickly," "The world is too small for me," "Everything for the greater glory of the Heart of Jesus," and so on. That world was mine. When I had entered the convent, everything seemed to me, for a moment, to be closing around me. now I could see that a great window was opening from which an infinite horizon could be sensed.

3

In the Tunnel of God

Meanwhile, other young people entered communities in Italy and Spain and came to Rome. Together we prepared to enter the novitiate, the period of most intense formation for taking vows to enter the Congregation. These young people came from very diverse places and situations. Those who had spent too much time in high schools or orphanages tended to bring into the religious life the behavior of their schools, resulting in problems and complicated situations — bad attitudes, depression, jealousies, affections for one or the other. Religious formation, therefore, had to deal with all these characteristics, which sapped much of the energy from proper religious life. But the Sisters didn't seem to be excessively concerned about this. They were accustomed to children and young people in their school, to people who had been brought up well, and to orphans. They knew these young people would know how to grow and mature if they truly had a vocation.

We arrived at the novitiate in late September of 1959, the year following my entry. The novitiate at that time was in Rieti, in a beautiful villa located on a hill a little outside the city. The large park with beautiful avenues of cypress and pine, and forests of fir and oak made the villa beautiful. It was surrounded by famous Franciscan places such as The Forest (which could be accessed from our villa), Fontecolombo, Poggiobustone and Greccio. But the house was uncomfortable, cold, and had been cobbled into a convent. The vast halls had become large dormitories where the beds were separated by white curtains. The other rooms were used, for better or worse, as a dining room, chapel, community room, and so on.

In novitiate I began to feel some difficulties which later became worse. The young Sisters and the more adult Sisters, who were about my age, were each trying in their own way to overcome their troubles in adapting. It was especially emotional problems that emerged. The Mother Teacher, Mother Genuine Scotti, was an excellent Sister of 72 years, very simple and open. Intuitive and tolerant, she did not understand how they chose her for that role. Sometimes she didn't really understand our problems. But I established a great a relationship with her, although I soon realized that it was useless to talk to her about my problems. In fact she believed that our spirit ought to be sober, without asking too many questions, and above all without getting into too much meticulous introspection. Today I think she was right, but I also think that the training should take place with a certain gradualness. It shouldn't go too fast. Of particular help to me was the vice-director, Mother Maria Rosa Parma, a young Sister who was intelligent and understanding. She was a little maternal, which was necessary for the very young Sisters.

Sister Maria Rosa left me quite free to grow and tried to get me to understand the spirit of the Congregation by bypassing aspects that were too rigid and were already creating problems for the Congregation itself. Given the differences in cultural, age and education as well as nationality, my difficulties with relationships weren't too obvious because we got along together well. I, in particular, had a certain verve and desire to play around. I had the ability to organize performances and parodies that lessened tensions that gradually arose. I wasn't too aware of that. Our recreations were often prolonged and a lot of fun, sometimes, because "the play wasn't finished yet." Once it occurred to me to put on *Arsenic and Old Lace*. Mother Maria Rosa, who encouraged this activity of mine, got the text for me. Each novice impersonated a character. Another novice and I had the more adult parts of two elderly ladies. It was a success that made us laugh for a week. The spectators were four professed Sisters, including the Mother Teacher. The Spanish Sisters barely spoke Italian, so sometimes they didn't understand what they were saying and broke lines in the wrong place. One of them had to say: "What is this mess?!" but said: "What is this? Mess. "We performed a range of other comedies, and tragedies, too, because where there were deaths there was more enjoyment. (Who knows why?) But there were also the famous series of performances to prepare for religious and liturgical festivals. In these cases, to escape banality, we tried to imitate television commercials and short sketches. Generally we made a spectacle of ourselves.

In this way, therefore, I quelled the difficulties that I felt inside, a range of information that I wasn't too convinced of, or rather, did not understand the usefulness of. Later I realized that some discipline, even in the smallest things, is of great benefit. The rules on cleanliness, order (everything in its place), abstinence from useless words, the mortification of one's own desire, curiosity, and the need to always voice one's opinion, helped to control one's self and one's own nature, especially mine, which has always been intrusive. The difficulties, however, were many, especially cohabitation. My young Sisters got along with me well. (At least I think so; later on I would realize my presumption). But they attributed my usual good mood to the fact that the Mother Teacher showed me a certain fondness. I don't know if it was true, but this was one of many points of conflict, even if nothing serious.

They always got sick on holidays and created a number of hinderances for small things: too much soap, the wimple put on wrong, the mess that got left somewhere. Many of those problems were revealed early in the vocational character. I didn't understand those things either, but I was tired because we were reciting a lot more prayers than prescribed, since the vocation of these Sisters was in the balance; resulting in shorter and shorter recreation periods of which I was a passionate supporter.

One day, at the height of intolerance, I said that there would be nothing strange about some people not having a vocation, and it would be better if they went back. It was an unfortunate sentence. They scolded me, and I had a great sense of guilt. Perhaps since I didn't want to pray, the poor Sisters wouldn't persevere. But, in general, I understood that there was something wrong. Once, having had to stay in bed with an intestinal ailment along with three other novices who were among the most restless, I was responsible for doing the spiritual reading, which included an exhortation of the founding mother. Usually this was done in the Community, and the Mother Teacher interrupted the reading occasionally to add ad hoc exhortations referring to specific cases of the Community. So I did too, but without making it clear that I was adding things from my head, referring to concrete cases. The poor novices who listened could not imagine how naughty I was, and they were amazed that the founding mother had an exhortation that applied just to our situation. They didn't even bother to learn where that strange reading came from.

To the Ends of the Earth

Certainly those weren't my only problems. I wanted to go on a mission. That's why I had become a missionary. And we were made to understand that everything was a mission; it wasn't necessary to leave Italy to be missionaries. I felt a need of other relationships. I rarely saw my family, for example, and visits were very regulated. My mother came to see me several times, and each time we were more reconciled, but I felt I needed to be with her longer and have various relationships—with people, with the parish, with my friends. I felt closed and limited. Only later would I realize the value of that year in retreat. Nor did I understand—it was less than two years since I'd joined—that everything needs time. I had started a process which involved continuous inner choices, choices which no one will ever know about. My prayer was dry and hard, but I did not understand that the God who had fascinated me would never leave me shut off from my fervid imagination. I had to travel a long interior road. I didn't know how risky it was. But, yes, I felt the discomfort that masks a disproportionate creative ability and an exorbitant need to joke and make people laugh. I really think it was excessive.

We came at last to the first religious profession. Testing, preparation, spiritual retreats, performances. As usual I had to prepare a sacred performance that we would put on before the Mother General and other people in the Institute. When the day came, the Mother and other Sisters were so tired that they fell asleep . . . during the performance. I was eager to take my vows because soon after that the mission I was longing for would come. My Mother Teacher, however, made the mistake of telling me that first I would be sent to teach in Turin, where seventy children were expecting me. I didn't like the idea. When I had entered, I had hidden the fact that for a long time I'd had my bachelor's certificate for teaching kindergarten. I'd hidden the fact because I had no intention of teaching. But then I was forced to turn over the documents. That news ruined the joy of the moment.

Despite everything, I cultivated inside myself the desire to connect myself to God, and finally, when I found myself lying on the ground under the black blanket that, as a ritual at the time, meant death to any desire for anything other than Him and His will, I understood that I was entering the tunnel of God. At that point, it was hard to get out of the tunnel. I knew, however, that I should not lose sight of the distant light that was attracting me so strongly.

4

Everything Is Mission

After my first profession, I was sent to Turin. It was late September. School had already begun. I liked Turin right away, and the fall made it fascinating. It was a bit shrouded by mist, and the trees were a thousand shades of color. As soon as I arrived I was sent, without pleasantries, to school. I was in a bad mood. I found a lot of children there. Those were the years of the great internal migration. Turin—our area in particular—was full of people from the South. In addition to nursery school children, after four in the afternoon I had to take care of all primary school children who hadn't gone home. Generally the parents came to pick up their children at 6:00, or even 7:00. It was hard work to keep them all together. The teachers were busy preparing for the next day or correcting homework. My voice went hoarse immediately but this did not change my situation.

The Sisters welcomed me with affection, but they made me understand that I had to make do. They had their own problems. I tried to deal with the exhaustion that overwhelmed me almost immediately. It had been just fifteen days since my professions of obedience, and I already found my first problems. But I got into the hectic pace of work. I unleashed my imagination to change the look of my little school. Away with artificial flowers, away with the ten saints' portraits, away with everything I knew to be old and inappropriate. Of course I quickly found trouble. *Who does she think she is, this young Sister who wants to change everything?* I even had the courage to write to the Mother General that that style of kindergarten wasn't up to standards. There weren't enough places for all the children, the furniture was old and unsuitable, the benches were uncomfortable, and so on. This horrified my elderly Superior. She told me, "You could at least talk to me first." She was right!

The other Sisters watched me and were a bit worried, partly about my health, partly because I appeared rather critical even if I did not speak. But we settled into a kind of solidarity. Generally we were very tired because we had kids from 6 a.m. to 7 p.m., and then we had to clean the whole school. When I arrived, one of the Sisters, the youngest, seemed to be quite cold to me. It was her character, but I understood that I had to stay in my space and not invade hers. I shouldn't be too friendly. But I accepted this kind of person rather passively, and I reacted with kindness. I asked "permission" to do things differently from the way she had established. She was slightly negative as a leader one had to depend on. My complacency towards her, or toward other Sisters for other reasons, was a choice. I didn't want more problems than I already had to deal with every day. There were many: my voice (I had to have a minor operation on my vocal cords); the children, who were terrible (I wasn't very patient!), and parents who were demanding, uncooperative, and gave the impression of abandoning the poor children at school.

And then there were the holidays. We needed to prepare performances for Christmas, Carnival, Mother's Day—a real marathon and often a real annoyance! On the first holiday I watched what the others were doing, and I was rather taken aback—marches, songs, and a recitation of the "Vispa Teresa." During the preparation for the next holiday I got involved in an obsessive preparation full of details that made me lose my mind. My little devils went crazy with joy: clothes, lanterns, balloons, dances, and a theater shows to the sound of classical music. The night before the party, already close to midnight, I was in a jumble of confusion. I was trying to organize things all alone. Suddenly, almost on tiptoe (it was her way of walking), Sister Fedele, entered the room. Sister Fedele was the one whom I had assumed to be disagreeable. She asked: "How far have we gotten?" I didn't answer. It was obvious that I was at a standstill and exhausted. Immediately she began to put everything in order, just asking when the first scene was, which things I had to use, etc. She made me an outline, organized everything in an exemplary way, moment by moment, by writing it clearly on a sheet of paper. She stayed with me until after two in the morning and before she left she said, "Tomorrow, at the time of the play, don't worry. I'll be with you to help." It was a lesson in behavior. Sympathy is not demonstrated by smiles. We became real Sisters. Since that day we organized parties together with a central theme and so many different things. I contributed my imagination, and she contributed her help.

To overcome the difficulty of keeping so many children busy, especially in the evening, I had to invent a lot of tricks that were particularly successful. Among these were a puppet theater and fairy tales performed in installments. With the help of Mother Emma Ross, who was a true artist, we made papier mâché and covered it with Vinavil and colors, creating a magnificent cast of puppets. In the late afternoon, confronted with a bunch of kids of all ages, I tucked myself into a little puppet theater with two or three boys. From there I used my voice to suggest how to imitate the ogre, the flour, Little Red Riding Hood.

Then we realized that, unfortunately, the children who were supposed to go home at five o'clock were staying until seven o'clock to see the theater, and those who usually did not stay in the afternoon, having heard about theater, stayed at school. That was a problem, too! Fairy tales, moreover, had the same effect. I dragged them out for twenty or thirty episodes, mixing Tom Thumb with Hansel and Gretel as well as with my imagination, remembering my mother's many stories. My voice, already sorely worn out by ten hours of school, received the coup de grace in the evening. Many times children returning to school said to me, "My mother, my dad said, 'what kind of story is she telling us?'" In fact, many of them returned home to repeat the episode to their parents, who were baffled by the mixed up stew that my imagination had cooked up.

Those seven years in Turin taught me many things. The Sisters, my companions, I loved from the heart. Mother Constance Bonavia was the director of the school, remarkable for her charity and her ability to pray. A priest, her friend, told us a few years later that while he was praying in church, he saw the lamp lit before the Blessed Sacrament suddenly go out. The first thing he thought in the face of this strange occurence was that "Madre Constance was dead." And that's just what happened. On that day and hour, Mother Constance died.

The gruff Mother Fedele, the one who had come to help me at midnight, had grown up without a mother, and all her life had dreamed of taking care of orphans. When she finally realized her dream, she died. She was not yet fifty years old. Sister Emma Rossi was very good at embroidery in gold and at painting. But then a congenital exhaustion made everything difficult for her. I convinced her to paint a bird of paradise, to freshen up the scenes of the theater, to paint the valances of a large living room, and to make a decoration with stylized flowers for the chapel. She said "no," but when I assured her I'd help her, she went to work. Then I cleverly confessed that I had never picked up a paintbrush. She fell into the trap and taught me a lot of things. Mother Piera Rossi was a French Sister. She was our pianist. She was in fragile health but kept up a very good mood. I drove her crazy making her write the music for songs that I had made up.

"But where did you get this song?" she asked. "There's no harmony!"

"You arrange it," I said.

The poor thing said, "Let's see...repeat ...."

I repeated with a different tone. By the end of the song she worked it out with a certain success.

Mother Clementina Raimondi was a real worker ant. We all worked a lot, but compared to her, we were merely grasshoppers. She knew to how to do everything and had a special ability to connect with people.

It was a great time, though I continued to struggle for my inner equilibrium. I had to channel my crazy imagination and organize my tumultuous emotions. The new Superior, Mother Jacinta Lupi, helped me a lot. She succeeded the elderly Mother Candida Antonietti, of whom I keep a reverent memory. Mother Jacinta helped me understand the essence of things. She was strict and sometimes uncompromising, but her intelligence and intuition helped me define some parameters within myself—not to radicalize my critical sense, to be a friend to myself, to love the people who seem not to deserve it, to not despair over mistakes. At the same time, Mother Jacinta made me aware of our Institute and how it was changing. She prepared me. Unfortunately this magnificent person wasn't always welcome. Sometimes her temperament was off-putting, but everyone appreciated her greatly.

In Turin I came to have positive relationships with the people, with the neighborhood, with the parish, and in some fashion with the culture. I enjoyed the Italia 61 exposition, the walks around town, and visits in the area. I started reading books by Jacques and Raissa Maritain, Leon Bloy, Van der Meer, Charles de Foucauld. I began to feed my mind and my heart, which I had not known how to calm down. God spoke to me in very different ways. I had to abandon the idea of finding God where I thought He should be, I had to lose my thought patterns. But it wasn't easy. A lot of time had to pass.

The year 1968 approached. From the institutional point of view, we had yet to enter the storm that was raging in the Church and some branches of the Institute, especially in the U.S. and in South America. But we sensed the youth movements and the new forms of catechesis in the sophisticated and abstruse questions that young priests were asking of first communion children, such as, "What is the most important moment of the Mass?"

The poor child began: "The consecration."

And the priest: "No!"

And the child: "Communion."

And the priest: "No."

In the end we were shocked because even we didn't know the answer. Finally the priest through an endless argument concluded, it is "In Christ, for Christ and with Christ"! Do you understand?

"No."

It was truly a time of confusion.

But we followed events closely. One day a young Jesuit priest, sent by the Holy See, came to visit us to explain that the Holy Father wanted our Institute to update itself, to open itself up, to renew itself, and that we should not offer resistance. We were shocked as we heard the words. We did not know what he meant. Our Superior was probably aware of everything, but she was not prepared for anything. We faced the situation calmly.

A few weeks later, two of our Sisters came from Milan and Rome and got us to understand the Institute's position on things. They urged us to cooperate by responding to questionnaires they had brought. They were Sister Imelda and Sister Chiara Grasselli, two wonderful people who later played an important role in the change and renewal of our Institute. Indeed, Mother Chiara would soon become our General Superior.

Meanwhile, a serious incident, this time familial, came to trouble days that were already difficult enough for me. My

Everything is Mission

mother was seriously ill. They sent me to Rome to visit her. I made the journey at night. It was the first time in six years that I was back in Rome. Since the end of the novitiate, my only trip had been to Pontremoli, in Tuscany, in the summer, every year, for a retreat. The trip seemed endless, even though I was traveling in the compartment with a Sicilian family whose Father, a man in his forties, was very cheerful and kept me entertained all night with his jokes and his remarks about other passengers. My traveling companion (back then we always traveled in pairs) slept soundly all night.

When we arrived at the Mother House in Rome, which I was entering for the first time, we found a lot of Institutional things had changed. I met one of our famous mothers, Mother Rosario Marchesi, who had been in Brazil for fifty years. She had met Mother Cabrini and was now almost blind.

She greeted me warmly and said, "You are young, but do not fear. Our Mother General is already planning to change some things in the Institute."

I still did not understand. Only later I learned that things had not turned out so simply. I went to Mother Edmonda, the Mother Superior who had received me the first time. I was told that she was ill. I went to visit her and found her very sad. She was one of the Sisters who was suffering a lot from the trauma of change. Greeting her, I asked if she remembered me. She replied with a smile, "How can I forget you?" I never saw her again. She died shortly afterwards.

Finally I was able to see my mother in San Camillo hospital. She was very serious and very lucid. My brother and my Sister took turns and never left her alone. At first I didn't understand she was dying. Tired of traveling and confused from so many events, it took me a while to catch on. My brother informed me of everything, and, in his usual way—he had always been a bit impetuous—concluded that the doctors were rude. Their behavior bothered him. The primary care doctor came into the room followed by a swarm of other doctors and students. Then he mumbled something and left. If a family member asked for information, he replied with a shrug. He clearly didn't know what to say, as always happens in these cases. I went back to Turin because there was no one to replace me at school. A few days later my Mother Superior came to see me in my cubicle. She hugged me and told me that my mother had died.

I did not return to Rome for the funeral, and later I regretted not having done so. This death made me suffer a lot, to the point that I thought that I would have no more desire to live. I wasn't excessively attached to my mother, but I adored her. As long as she was well, I did not mind if she was far away, but from that moment on, I felt an abysmal distance that separated me from her, and I sank into mortal sadness.

That same summer I had to go to Pontremoli for a month to get ready for my perpetual vows. It was a month of great distress. I prayed: "Out of the depths I cry to you O Lord, Lord hear my voice ...." But I had no consolation. The environment around me was affected now that we were going through the transition. There was no one I could entrust my anguish to. I remember one day, at the height of desolation, I prayed to the Madonna: "Virgin Mary, if I have to continue like this, it is better to die immediately. Should I do the mission, helping people to live, to hope? In these conditions?" I do not know what happened. Certainly nothing extraordinary, but after some time, I was filled with a certainty—my mother was alive. In another way, sooner or later, I would see her again. And I had an intuition: eternity.

5

1968: University and Vatican II

At the end of the summer of 1968 I received my first transfer. They sent me to Sant'Angelo Lodigiano, the town where Mother Cabrini was born.

The mission was very lively. There was an orphanage, a nursery and primary school, and parish activities. I was very sorry to leave Turin, and, especially, my dear Sisters. But I didn't even have time to cry. Sant'Angelo gave me one of the kindergarten sections. The novice director who had preceded me had taken everything away except the benches. Mother Virginia Maria Riva, a young and very nice Sister, immediately came to help.

She said, "Don't worry, what's mine is yours. We'll help."

To the Ends of the Earth

They also assigned me to help Sister Leocadia, who was employed by the largest orphanage, called Profetta. Keeping all those children disciplined was difficult for me. They had various behavioral problems. When I was with them, they were all excited, jumping and shouting, and I couldn't calm them down with my only method available: fairy tales. These girls were older, so to keep their attention, I had to invent a lot of different love plots with happy endings. In the evening, after the prayers, the children were supposed to go to sleep, but it was useless. There was no way. They were talking, laughing, and constantly asking to go to the bathroom.

Then I walked down the two aisles of the dormitory—there were three long rows of beds— telling stories. The silence was immediate. After a few days, Sister Leocadia, amazed at the silence, came to see me and chided me. It was nice, she said, but I was spoiling the girls. When I was no longer there, she would not be able to continue. She had her own way to keep them calm: she put her finger to her mouth and made a long "*Shsssss,*" and they all fell silent.

Our Superior was a grand woman, tall, very intelligent, and a bit authoritarian. From her, in the opinion of the Sisters, one never got anything, especially for the school. We had to work wonders with the teaching materials, exercise books, games and so on. One day I went to talk to her. I explained that in Turin the school was much more advanced. There were plenty of Froebelian and Montessori teaching materials. Here the kids

1968: University and Vatican II

were crazy because we had no way to make them work. In Turin we did exhibitions and studied drawing. In short, I exaggerated a little and concluded that if there was no money for a decent school, I could write to the Mother General.

The poor Superior looked at me curiously. "Tusa," she said, "there is no need to write to the Mother General. Come with me to Brescia on Monday."

When the other Sisters heard this, they couldn't believe it. In Brescia we went to the store of a publisher called La Scuola, where they sold everything under the sun for children. I picked out slates, colored paper, crayons and markers, games and everything that appealed to me, all before the astonished eyes of the Superior who, after hearing my reasons, paid for it all. She said, "But this stuff is not just for you, it's for everyone."

"Yes, yes, it's for everyone."

This incident convinced me that the fear of facing situations was creating a lot of problems in the Convent that I had never suffered. Even if it was a lot of work, it established good relationships among the Sisters. And with the people in the town there was a happy understanding.

In the evening, after school, when we were very tired and we had a little free time, we went for a visit to the birthplace of Mother Cabrini. We crossed the whole town and arrived at the little house. There we were met by two kindly Sisters who came each morning and returned in the evening to accommodate pilgrims who came to pray. The two Sisters, now elderly, were

To the Ends of the Earth

Sister Antoinette, the Spanish Sister who used to entertain us with her stories of the Civil War when we first entered the novitiate, and Sister Saverio Suardi, another amiable missionary. They were preparing coffee with a little cognac, with the famous "amaretti Gallina" liqueur," whose flavoring came from the courtyard of the Saint's house. In the kitchenette, with fireplace lit, we talked about of this and that, the novelty of Vatican II, the new style of liturgy that our chaplain would not admit. The warmth that these two Sisters radiated also spread to people who did no more than visit Mother Cabrini's house.

Sister Antoinette died some years later in Milan. She was lucid, and I had the good fortune to see her again. When death approached, she was so happily radiant that all the staff of the clinic went to see her. She said: "Come, come, my groom. I have been waiting all my life!" (She said *bieni, bieni,* instead of *vieni vieni,* because being Spanish she could not make the sound "v".) Mother Saverio was a great missionary in Argentina and Nicaragua. She herself told me that once, in Nicaragua, the Apostolic Nuncio had invited all the religious for an inspirational talk, and then in the room there was a great silence. The minutes passed. No one spoke. Then suddenly she, with her great big voice, exclaimed: "Excellent, Sisters, this seems like a funeral wake." At that, everyone began to laugh, and began to speak without hesitation. People still remember it today.

With the Oratory we always had hundreds of girls in the

1968: University and Vatican II

courtyard and in the halls. They danced the Charleston and the cha-cha-cha terribly but lively. The Sisters were truly integrated with each other and with everyone. I was a little less so. But people considered "the monastery" (so called because our house was an old monastery) as their home. There was an a extraordinary apostolic and pastoral climate, and no one could predict that soon we would be entering a crisis.

I, as usual, was rather critical of how we took care of the orphans. The methods were not the ideal of pedagogy and psychology. There were many things I did not like. I had several discussions with the Superior and with the Sisters, but my objections had no effect.

I stayed in Sant'Angelo for less than a year. During the summer I met our new Superior General, Mother Clare Grasselli, at Pontremoli. I had met her in Turin and then I heard people talk about her. I felt a little uncomfortable when I began to speak, but then, during the conversation, I realized that I had found someone very different from the other Sisters. She was simple, transparent, intelligent, friendly, humble and strong. With her, one could talk about everything. She had beautiful green eyes, and was always smiling and serene. I did not imagine at that time that this person would be the protagonist of a key passage in the history of our Congregation. Her appearance did not betray the complexity of the problems that she had to confront. We talked of many things. She urged me not to be afraid to express my opinions, to use my talents, to try to understand the times we were going through, to deepen our spirituality.

When I returned to Sant'Angelo they told me that I had been transferred again. I was going to Pontremoli to continue my studies. I was sorry to leave that place so soon. I was fond of the land, the people, the mission.

In Pontremoli I immediately got into my studies. They told me that if I was able, I would have to do a marathon—four years in a year and a half—attending regular courses to prepare for the exams. Then, with an average score of eight, I could enter the superior courses. Resuming studies was hard on me—not for any inability but because I was still in a phase of psychological uncertainty. I needed to be with people, to invent possibilities, to gauge my weaknesses and energy. To spend hours and hours sitting and devouring books required a lot of effort. Luckily I found excellent Sisters: Sr. Gemma, Sr. Benigna and Sr. Emidia, who later became a great friend. They all helped me, but I think they underestimated my difficulties. In the evening they sent me to recreation with terrible girls from inside the school who were very rambunctious, mainly trying to communicate with the boys outside the school. With them I could not tell tales, but I pretended to be a graphologist. I read their handwriting, and then, giving a look like a witch, I read their palms. If I was able to guess eighty percent of the facts (it wasn't hard), they brought me the handwriting of their boyfriends, and so I was able to keep them in check. But, I got

1968: University and Vatican II

through that wearisome year and, with dignity enough, managed to get my teaching diploma.

At the end of September I was transferred to Rome.

In the Mother House I encountered a bit of chaos. The youngest Sisters (juniors) were entrusted to me, as was, indirectly, the Mother House. (The assistant general continued to maintain her role as director of the House). Vatican II had come in like a whirlwind, creating a certain disorganization in the traditional ways of doing things. But now one could pray in new ways, speak more freely, take initiatives. Sisters could go out alone. They could buy their personal things for themselves and visit friends and relatives. Sisters arrived from Argentina, Brazil, the United States to study or to take refresher courses outside of Rome at a congregation House called Mundo Migliore. Moreover, Sisters from other congregations were hosted from Africa, India or Latin America. The novices were regarded very differently. They came and went freely. The austere and silent way of life that I had found when I entered had disappeared. It took a little work to readjust oneself. Our superiors were tolerant. They understood that it was a time of transition that we had to face with maturity. Some years before we had changed our habits. Now we were dressed in short, gray dresses, kind of cute (minus the jacket, which no one liked and was worn very little). Also, our veil was gray and light. The American Sisters arrived with various styles of dress and colors, including black and white, black and gray, and white and gray. In short, there was room to have fun.

In that chaos, the full and harmonious figure of the General Superior, Mother Chiara, stood out. She was a point of reference. She tolerated diversity but not extravagance. She continuously motivated our charity and deepened our charism. It was then that I began to better understand our spirit. Up to that point I had lived without a reason. Now I began to understand its value. Mother Chiara had us study theology, liturgy, and Sacred Scripture, and she invited all the Sisters who were able to improve their studies and their missionary preparation. So the Mother House was filled with many "student" Sisters between 30 and 50 years old. We had to help each other because everyone had difficulties. I remember a Sister old enough that, when she managed, after several weeks, to understand the Pythagorean theorem, she began to clap her hands and jump for joy. I started a two-year vocational psychology program at the Salesian University. Even there I found an atmosphere of great dispute. Some professors had been replaced for having ideas that were too progressive, and students (mostly young priests) challenged the decision. Other religious had left the Congregation and were still attending the university. My fellow students were arguing about everything and everyone, for or against one trend or another. On the advice of one of my professors, I invited a young priest to preach at a retreat for our young Sisters. Fortunately, after coming to know about his ideas, I had time to cancel the commitment.

1968: University and Vatican II

However, I became fond of psychology. It especially helped me understand myself, my reactions, my feelings, my tendencies, and the reasons for the many emotions that affected my personality. I had some very good teachers. I concluded two years and I wanted to continue with higher education courses, but the Rector told me I needed a degree or at least to be enrolled at the university. I talked to my superior and she encouraged me to matriculate in the university. I enrolled at the Magisterium Maria Assunta, which at that time was still frequented mostly by Sisters. The program took four years. I studied and did many other things. I remained in charge of the Mother House with serious overlapping problems. I continued to take care of the young Sisters, again with many problems caused by my differences with my superiors regarding the training criteria. And I tried to study in order to take my exams in June with a high average that would allow me fee exemptions. This was not requested by anyone, but to me it seemed like an obligation.

At the Magisterium I found excellent professors, and here, too, I did not lack conflicts because of my divergent opinions, especially from the religion professor, who used the podium to criticize all the movements he disagreed with. One day I jumped up and left the classroom. The Rector sent for me and very gently scolded me. It was an excellent opportunity to express my opinions on the university which otherwise satisfied me well enough.

I didn't form many relationships. The Sisters seemed too concerned about the studies and the grades, except for a few. I had enrolled in pedagogy, and I was passionate about philosophy. But I remember my great trouble understanding Hegel. There was a young Sister who talked about Hegel the way I talked about my stories. One day I decided to let her explain him to me. She was very good. In half an hour she got me to understand what Hegel meant. Then she told me to pray for her. A few months later she was out of her congregation.

In those years we were hard hit by the premature death of our General Superior, Mother Chiara. For me it was another terrible blow after the pain I'd felt at the death of my mother. I had put a lot of hope in Mother Chiara. I wished that our Institute would rise up and take back its missionary audacity, reaching a balance and resuming the missionary prophecy Mother Chiara had started. Her illness affected me intensely. With another Sister, Sister Rosario Compagner, a dear Brazilian Sister with whom I had became friends right away, I went into seclusion to pray, did novenas, made pilgrimages and sacrifices. At that time Father Massimiliano Kolbe was beatified. I went to St. Peter's for the event and for a long time I stood there with my eyes closed, insistently pleading for the miraculous recovery of Mother Chiara. I wanted this miracle at all costs! Mother Chiara died on November 20 of that same year, in Milan. A few days earlier we were going with the juniors to Sant'Angelo Lodigiano, where the twenty-five year anniversary of Mother Cabrini's

1968: University and Vatican II

sainthood was being celebrated. We passed by the Columbus clinic, where Mother Chiara was hospitalized. She smiled at me and praised me to the young Sisters. It was impossible for me to say one word. She died a few weeks later. It was an irreparable loss. We cried for her a long time.

In the meantime, Mother Lucia Victor Rodriguez ran the Institute. She was a smart and resourceful Brazilian Sister who was planning to take me with her to visit South America—Brazil and Argentina. I believe that no one in the General Council agreed, but she did not listen to reason. It was my first intercontinental trip. I enjoyed that trip a lot. It tempered my sorrow at the death of Mother Chiara a little. I was enchanted with the beauty of Rio de Janeiro and Brazil in general. I also saw, for the first time, Argentina. None of the Sisters understood the reason for my journey, but at the time many strange things were happening that I didn't understand. What puzzled me, however, was the kind of life that I found. There was a lot of confusion; biased tendencies, some with the traditional, some with the new order of things: exaggerations on both sides. Many Sisters left the convent, others asked for a leave of absence, others went into seclusion. In Argentina, at the time, the situation was not much different. A few months later the Mother Teacher left with all the novices.

When I returned to Rome I was still a little disturbed, but the General Chapter conference was being prepared to elect the new General Superior and the new Council. I was appointed

Chapter delegate, and I attended the General Chapter. It was 1972. The experience helped me to understand cultural differences. We Italians, in general, struggle to have clear rules: *This must be done, this should not be done.* The American Sisters had more open rules. They left people free. One day an elderly and very intelligent American Sister took me aside and told me: "You're so young, why are you so rigid?" I gave her all the possible reasons, to which she replied: "You know what happens? You Italians set 'rules' and then don't follow them, while we Americans don't want rules because we know what we have to do."

It was true. A few years later I realized this. She also served to understand Mother Chiara's struggle and her great effort to nurture unity in diversity. Those were difficult times. Sister Regina Casey, an American, was elected General Superior. She was moderate and intelligent, and she continued the revival. She had received a difficult legacy.

I devoted myself, meanwhile, to continuing my studies. I prepared to defend my thesis, which I was impassioned with. It was on the influence of Jacques Maritain on Italian culture. He had just died. I met with many people and interviewed friends of the late philosopher. After that I had to dedicate myself to training and vocational ministry, of which much was said but little was done. Meanwhile, they continued the process of modernization. The Communities must be smaller, and in smaller Houses, especially abroad. In Italy the news didn't

1968: University and Vatican II

really take root. But this process of change was to last much longer. Gradually, however, things came back to normal, even though there were obvious contradictions between tradition and progress, between fidelity to the old and fidelity to the new. In any case, it was a matter of two fidelities. There was one special problem: our theological thinking. For the most part we were molded in pre-Vatican II patterns and were struggling to take on the emerging new theology and ecclesiology. They changed so many external things, but the mindset remained the same. It happened that even in the new mode of prayer, for example, we stuck with the fixed thought patterns of the much-criticized old style lest someone impose their new ideas on us, and the situation of the past repeated. Missionary life, however, went forward. There were new communities in Africa, in Lebanon, in the new immigration areas such as Switzerland, Luxembourg, England.

A few days before I was to defend my thesis, my Superior General called me to tell me of my next transfer, once I'd graduated. I was to go to Central America, and I would work in education in Nicaragua and Guatemala.

First Intermission

When you hear the inner call to enter the religious life, you do not have the slightest idea what might happen. The only light that in some way guides us is the certainty (and even this is very fragile) that God calls us via certain human intermediations.

The awareness of being only at the service of an ideal makes its way inside us, very gradually. The first stage of this process involves an enormous expenditure of energy. We believe that a lot depends on our own efforts, above all when we strive to realize some project that our fantasy or imagination has produced. This applies to the concept of mission, both the concept of holiness and, even more, the concept of God.

Inner growth consists, essentially, of the labor to "dismantle" our projects, to make room for the Holy Spirit to build

His. This sounds easy in words, but it is very complex because it has to do with our personality, our culture, the education we received and, in general, our ability to understand, to perceive, to create. All the gifts we receive from God—intelligence and creativity, culture or tendencies—can work in favor of our Christian fulfillment and therefore God's plan, but also work against it.

They work in favor when we, freely, accept the risk of questioning all our certainties, losing them or changing them, to then find them again, purified and reorganized according to a new value system. They work against it when our resistance to change and our fear of "getting lost" is strong enough to discourage any attempt by our will. What does our inner strength depend on when we risk—or don't risk—all that we are, all that we desire, all that we do? It is always a mystery. But we can think, in general, that it depends on the grace of God, the consistency of our ideals, a morsel of desire for adventure, and certain natural tendencies that fuel the engines of all the people who seriously set objectives for themselves.

In my case it seems mysterious that, despite some real difficulties, I have never had the desire to go back. The exterior difficulties have not been, for me, insurmountable. I refer, for example, to the need to adapt to different people, cultures, work, climate, and different cuisines all the time; also to the fact that almost always my ideas didn't line up with those of others; the fact that I have always had a critical view of the mentality and of

First Intermission

the internal organization of the convent and to my tendency to be different in an organization that values stability and uniformity.

My most serious difficulties have always been of a psychological nature, or even an ideal nature. These difficulties would probably give me problems anyway had I formed a family or been able to accomplish my initial projects.

The process that I have called "interior dismantling," however, was hard. There were very few people who could seriously help me, and therefore I had to establish an absolutely personal relationship with God, who had fascinated me and taught me, against my will, about loneliness, inner silence, emptiness, and my impotence to change my destiny in any way. The darkness to which my faith has always been subordinated has enabled me not to hesitate long in the face of the demands of the Gospel, and to force me to distinguish between what pleased me and what concerned Christian values. Errors and weaknesses should not look for unfounded excuses; rather, they should look for mercy mercy.

I spent a lot of energy bridging the gap between the ideal that I proposed and my inconsistencies. But I also realized that this task was more from God's grace than from mine. I abandoned myself to Him, hoping in His mercy (though it would not have been necessary to hope). The conflict within myself would weaken after several years of religious life. I must say, though, that it has never disappeared. At the same time, the continuous balance-imbalance or chaos always arose from the richness and vitality of my life. Through various existential moments (which lasted years), I realized even better that the mission is a gift. Furthermore, it doesn't depend on us. We can work, pray, struggle, and die to achieve a goal, but, as the Scripture says in Psalm 127: "Unless the Lord build the house, in vain do its builders labor [...] in vain you rise early and go to bed late, toiling for food to eat—for the Lord gives sleep to those he loves."

Now what would so much suffering, sacrifice, renunciation and struggles be good for? It is to be friends with God, to have that which we sought in him, to have it in our sleep (as the Psalm says), that is, when He—not we— wishes it, an active, vigilant, overwhelmingly heroic participation takes place, because we and others we can have "life in abundance" (cfr. John 10:10). This is not to say that what you do is useless. It means that the essential lies in being rather than in doing. If we received from Mother Nature a natural disposition that is very capable of production, this gift must go through many purifications if it is not to be constantly frustrated. And if we have received a meditative or contemplative disposition, that which could be laziness must be filtered out from what is true contemplation.

Having had God as principal educator, I went through all kinds of frustrations. God's guidance is a magnificent train track on which truth and justice, charity and hope, and all sorts of virtues run. All that derails from this track creates terrible frustrations, and this is a perfect form of education.

My desire to attain holiness has been very purified. God knows

First Intermission

what we need. He does not accept advice. Slowly but inexorably, all we have so fearfully risked finds its proper place. The faith that grows unifies all the scattered insights within us. The difficulty is that because of the fragmentary nature of our religion, the Catholic faith raises endless questions in nonbelievers. God, One and Three, the Church, the sacraments, the Bible, devotions, and morality—they lose consistency when you start to feel that "only one thing is necessary" and that the only commandment is "to love God above all things and our neighbor as ourselves" and that we must "seek first the kingdom of God and his righteousness, and the rest will be given unto you."

All this, then, is not separate from everyday life, from the effort to get along with others, from the need to earn a living by the labor of your hands, and the disillusionment that reality brings to everyone. And it is precisely in this solidarity that we walk with the good and evil of the world, supporting each other, accepting the mystery of a life full of uncertainties, but also the womb of infinite possibilities that God's plan provides us.

6

Opting for the Poor or for Communism?

In July of 1974 I arrived in Nicaragua with a group of novices. It was what they called tropical winter, a season of rains and, worse, a terrible hurricane called Fifí. The tail of this storm struck Nicaragua for several days and nights. I was frightened by the violence of the rain, the wind, the water coming in everywhere, the mold in my shoes, suitcase, and clothes. I remembered what I had read in Gabriel García Márquez's *One Hundred Years of Solitude*. But when calm returned, everything changed. The tall palm trees glistened in the sun, and the nearby forest displayed an endless array of magnificent greens.

To the Ends of the Earth

Fascinated as I was by the novelty of it all, I felt no immediate cultural shock. It's true that everything was different, but something we had in common united us, and the sense of being in the Cabrinian family eased my entry. Nicaragua was still traumatized by the earthquake of December, 1972, which had destroyed the whole older part and most of the new part of Managua. There were many dead, and even our big high school, which we had just finished building, collapsed.

They told me that I was to take care of the education of the young Sisters and girls who wanted to become Sisters as well as the future novices. To facilitate the task of acculturation, I took part in a course for educators organized by the Latin American Conference of Religious (CLAR) in Guatemala, where I was to live. Toward the end of the year, therefore, I went to Guatemala with two other Sisters. This program was, for me, enlightening and shocking. That's where I came to understand the Latin American situation.

As was common in Latin America, the methodology of the program consisted of the presentation of the social, political, cultural, economic and ecclesiastical reality in each Latin American country the participating members came from. There were more than 150 participants representing 18 countries. Given the synthesis of elements common to this multinational reality, we were dedicated to much reflection and prayer. Then we were shown the evangelical and theological aspects and those aspects which fell within the role of education.

OPTING FOR THE POOR OR FOR COMMUNISM?

The reality presented us with the situation of the poor, the institutionalized injustice, and the marginalization of indigenous peoples, women, the weak, and the oppressed. We were shown the corruption of military dictatorships, the starvation wages, and the trampling of the most basic human rights. Theological reflection clarified the option to help the poor, to defend the voiceless, to denounce injustice, and to bring hope to so many desperate people. The training had to nurture awareness and bring about change. The traits of liberation theology was clear, and therefore the CLAR was viewed with suspicion by governments and even by those of a certain mentality in the Catholic Church. I awoke suddenly from my cultural sleep. I was terribly impressed by everything I was hearing even when it expressed criticism of the European culture that had brought colonization. And the Church and those of the religious life were not exempt from guilt. Their methods were pro-slavery and indirectly supported the policies of the oppressors.

It took me a long time to digest all of this. The program lasted almost two months. At the time, all I could do was roll up my sleeves because my mission was beginning. The relationship with other religious men and women helped me a lot. We immediately established an inter-congregational Center for young people who were preparing for religious life. I was able to use my degree in psychology, my education in pedagogy, and everything I knew. Others helped me in group dynamics, leading a film club, preparing work schedules—all with a beginner's level of Spanish even though I had studied a few years at the university.

Soon I came to realize that the information received in the course of the CLAR sessions was not only true, but it was only a faint picture of reality. Going into the actual, real-life situation, I realized that I had only superficial knowledge. The military dictatorships, the persecution of priests and religious, of catechists and all those who opted to help the poor, was always justified with accusations of communism. Among those who died were politicians, trade unionists, intellectuals, journalists, common people, and anyone who dared to ask for a minimum of rights.

These situations touched us closely, and I began to understand the rift that divided the Church itself. I met many liberation theologists, as they were called, really good, humble, generous priests, many of whom were killed or abducted and "disappeared." They were difficult years marked by many beautiful and different experiences that are beyond telling and that changed my way of thinking.

Three events emerge above all from this rich experience: the earthquake in Guatemala in 1976, the Sandinista revolution in Nicaragua in 1979, and the experience of our mission in Matiguás, Nicaragua.

7

Earthquake in Guatemala

One evening, in Nicaragua, I was with some novices on the terrace of one of our vacation cottages. The cottage was a little rudimentary but it was right on the shore of the Pacific Ocean. The sea was dark with little sparkles from fishing boats. A nearly full moon illuminated a strip of sea, and the waves were getting louder and louder because the tide was rising. It was close to midnight, and it was terribly warm. Suddenly a young novice said, "I don't know what's wrong with me, but tonight I'm afraid of the sea." Others joined her, each with her fear. I didn't say anything because I'm always afraid. I tried to understand what they were feeling. They thought the sea, the moon with the halo of clouds, and other impressions were strange. We went to bed worried.

TO THE ENDS OF THE EARTH

The next morning, at about five o'clock, Sisters of our nearby house, in Diriamba, informed us that there had been a terrible earthquake in Guatemala: I had to leave immediately.

I ran home, quickly packed a suitcase and went to the airport. In less than an hour you could reach Guatemala City—if you found the right plane. The Managua airport was full of people, but no one was able to give precise information. Some said one thing, some another. At our House in Guatemala there were two Sisters, Mother Paul, who was rather elderly, and Sister Gloria, a young Sister. I arrived in Guatemala City that same morning.

A strange silence gave me the impression of a cemetery. The taxi took me home through a completely deserted city. I asked the taxi driver for news. He was very vague. He said that the epicenter of the earthquake was in the north, in Chiché and he named other regions. As we passed through the center of town, I began to see the destruction caused by the earthquake. From the road you could see facades completely detached from the rest of the house, letting us see the interiors with unmade beds heaped up, tilted wardrobes, kitchens and furniture in confusion. The closer we got to the neighborhood of our home, the more we could see collapsed houses and rooms that looked like rhombuses rather than squares or rectangles. Towards the periphery of the city, houses were razed to the soil, the more so because they were made of mud and pieces of wood. Given the great silence and the complete absence of people I asked the

Earthquake in Guatemala

taxi driver: "But the people, where are they?" He replied that they had fled.

Our house, a fairly new building constructed close to a little church not yet finished, was apparently standing, but one part was uninhabitable because it was leaning, and another part had a two-story wall completely detached from the rest. I found Mother Paul crying, sitting on a chair on the sidewalk of the house in front of ours. Between tears and interjections— "the horror, the horror!"—she told me that at three in the morning—the time remained famous because all the clocks of the churches that had collapsed had stopped at that time—she heard a loud crash as deafening as thunder. She woke up. It took her a moment to understand. She got up and went around the room without realizing where she was. She thought she was near the window. She felt a curtain and it gave way under her hands. She was directly in front of the door into the hallway.

Finally she understood that it was an earthquake. (Less than two years earlier she had lived through the one in Managua.) She tried to get out, shouting the name of another Sister as well as screaming "Lord, Lord, what did I tell you last night?" The younger Sister later told me that just the evening before, she had asked the Lord to be spared another earthquake because they had already lived through three in Nicaragua.

After they managed to get out through the rubble of the house, Mother Paul realized that what she had thought was the curtain of the window was the wall of the house that was completely detached. The partition walls of the rooms had all fallen. The foundation was badly loosened, putting everything else in danger. Only the kitchen and the laundry room downstairs seemed to hold. We could have sued the builder of the house. He had built it to anti-seismic specifications, but in his own way—however we refrained from doing so because he later rebuilt it at a good price. If we had all been in the house, it certainly would have been a tragedy. We attributed our good fortune to Mother Cabrini's grace and the prayers of Mother Paul.

Sister Gloria ended the story about that night with curious episodes, such as the disappearance of all the cats, the fact that the dog, which was tied up, had broken the chain and run away, and also the solidarity of people who immediately rushed to see what had happened to the Sisters. The poor neighborhood adjacent to ours, la Reina ("the Queen"), was razed to the ground. The poor houses all plunged into a ravine. They had been built illegally, so the poor had tried to build them in the most inaccessible areas of old chasms, really the sides of cliffs that had been created by previous earthquakes. This was to avoid landowners forcing them away. But as soon as they wore a little path and planted something, someone always seemed to drive them off.

From that night for a long time, we slept in our Fiat minivan in the square near the house. We had to stay close because looting had started. Early in the morning, people knocked on

Earthquake in Guatemala

the window and offered us a cup of coffee from a thermos. Later we camped on a corner of the house with a camp stove. We spent the first few months putting ourselves at the service of Caritas and the Red Cross. We would spend the whole day distributing food and clothes, sheets of galvanized iron to rebuild roofs, and clothes that Caritas gave us. We often got a lot of laughs because we wanted to throw away gilded shoes with stiletto heels or designer evening dresses. But when the poor earthquake victims saw such fancy clothes, they were dying to have them, so we let them choose what they wanted.

What shocked me most was the behavior of the government. Through television and the radio you heard slogans like Guatemala is up on its feet - as if to say, *Don't worry, nothing happened!* Then a Sister of a local congregation said she had gone to the countryside that same day to see what had become of her family. After three days of endless difficulties she managed to reach the village. The roads were blocked by landslides. Incredibly, entire villages had disappeared. When she reached her village, she found that not only was it gone but there was a pile of rubble several meters high in the middle of which the bodies of those who were not able to escape, especially the elderly and children, were left buried. The poor Sister returned to Guatemala City in dismay. She met with members of the government on radio and television and shouted about the dramatic situation in the north. Rescue operations were triggered (in a manner of speaking, because the delay was bewildering) almost a week after the disaster.

So the routine of our lives changed. The novices returned to Guatemala and, in groups, we put ourselves at the disposal of the emergency centers. The Conference of Religious of Honduras sent a large truck equipped with some facilities for emergency situations. The cab of the truck was separated by a large window, and the rest of the vehicle had spaces for sleeping, celebrating Mass, showing films with speakers, and even heat a little water or make coffee. Two novices and I drove that truck around the whole earthquake zone for two months. The purpose of the mission was to revive the indigenous people, who were the hardest hit. They thought that God had punished them for doing something wrong. This interpretation was spread by Protestant sects who insisted on the fact. The poor natives were terrified, the more so because they had been persecuted by the government because one of their leaders had struggled to get them assigned ownership of the land they had cultivated for thirty years. During these tours we explained our program and invited people to participate.

Every day we held reflection meetings, played games with the children (in which the adults also took part), gave out some information on prevention hygiene, and did a little schooling. In the evening we showed films. It was amazing how many people would gather and how much they liked the movies! The show consisted of a film about the life of Jesus, a languid Mexican version; a little film forum in which people participated wonderfully, and a comedy that amused them enormously. Somehow we ate and slept, but we lived in the same precarious situation as the people. I had the courage to put on my pajamas every night, having to sleep on the floor inside the truck. Our big drama was the toilet. Generally it was organized like a latrine in the midst of cornfields, close to a cemetery. When we needed to go at night, we always went out together because the novices saw ghosts all around us.

Our experience after the earthquake was both terrible and wonderful. Terrible because I came to know the extreme poverty and marginalization of these people. It was wonderful because I got to know the dignity of the indigenous people, their traditions, their magnificent craftsmanship, their ability to suffer, to forgive, and to keep hoping. Often I was impressed by the fact that some of the parish priests we met on the trip—certainly not all—were more concerned about the fallen church than about the people living in conditions of extreme hardship. I remember a Belgian Father became a master builder to rebuild, with the people, the whole village in a better place. He taught the poor to help each other (everyone had to work together on every home). He called the new village "Exodus." And of course it was frowned upon by the government.

The reconstruction of the House and the reorganization took us more than a year, but it was a period rich in events and innovations—along with some tropical diseases, parasites and amoebas—and finally I came to better understand what "opting for the poor" meant. I lost my prejudices, my false defenses, my justifications. I had to admit that my European mentality had to be converted, and those experiences were a privileged way. They didn't change my behavior or my habits or my character, but they changed the way I think, pray, love, and judge. The world of the poor went through me like a hurricane. I began to appreciate the new culture that had welcomed me. The insecurity that I had to get used to led me to understand that in this country, everything is precarious and fragile. Very few things are solid.

When I returned to Italy some time later, I immediately felt myself somewhat a foreigner. The Sisters weren't too interested in my experiences and, moreover, there was no lack of problems also in Italy—the Red Brigades, earthquakes, kidnappings. They didn't have much time for me. I stayed there longer than expected due to a microbe that developed and caused tonsillitis. I had to have my tonsils removed, and then I got phlebitis.

I was quite satisfied to return to Central America. I took no end of suitcases because now I knew what I absolutely could not find there. I resumed my activities with more vigor.

8

Revolution in Nicaragua

With the trauma of the earthquake in Guatemala just passed, another crucial moment in the history of Central America was brewing.

On my mission, I often traveled between Guatemala and Nicaragua. Sometimes I used the plane, sometimes a bus going from Mexico to Costa Rica, but by bus I was forced to sleep in El Salvador. The trip by land involved six border crossings—one to leave Nicaragua, two for Honduras, two for El Salvador, and one for Guatemala. Sometimes we made the journey driving ourselves in our Fiat minivan. It was always in need of repair due to the poor condition of the roads and the heat. Border controls were increasingly picky, obsessive, meticulous. The guards were terrible. They often confiscated whatever they found and then shared it among themselves. They looked through our underwear, opened envelopes, read books that we brought, often without understanding anything. They said that we Sisters were carrying subversive material. When we came to Nicaragua, the control was even worse. Customs had photographs of undesirables. A Salesian priest who could not enter Nicaragua disguised himself each time in a different way: once a rich gentleman, once a bearded intellectual, another time a laborer. Once he managed to get across the border of Costa Rica or Honduras, and he managed to get away with other things. Many priests were in the same situation.

One of our missions in Nicaragua was in the eastern district of the city, a district considered "hot" because there were two very lively parishes attended by many young people. One of the parishes was ours. The parish church was right in our house. It was a large hall that was used for many things. It was filled with young people who were often protesting the injustices committed by the dictator's National Guard. Many young people were put in prison for protesting or because they were caught reading a poster, or because they were found in possession of a photograph of Che Guevara, Camilo Torres, or even worse, Fidel Castro.

Another very dramatic period began, of unending crimes. They "disappeared" people, especially young people, who were tortured, the girls raped, then killed. In one famous symbolic act, the Somoza government wanted to make an exemplary lesson of a young ex-soldier who had gone over to the *Frente Sandinista*. He was thrown alive from a helicopter into the jaws of an active crater, the volcano Masaya. His name was David Tejada Peralta. Most of our young Sisters, especially those who were attending university or high school, were involved in the liberation movement, but it was never known to what extent. The other Sisters, especially the Spanish ones, did not agree with this involvement. They could not help but remember the Spanish Civil War.

It was just at this time we opened a new mission in a rural area near the border with Honduras. The land was owned by large landowners, and peasants were living in extreme poverty. In our visits around the region, we learned of many unjust situations. The people were at the mercy of some local authorities who had power of life and death. No one rebelled. The level of awareness in the rural areas was very low. I knew the humanistic activities of some good priests, mostly foreigners. Especially American Fathers struggling, with a lot of energy, for the poor. The government tolerated them because of its relations with the United States. I remember a tall, thin Father who organized a movement of catechists for the rural area. The Somozista guards, unable to do anything to the Father because he was North American, instead imprisoned and tortured his young people. He stirred up a scandal, complained to the dictator, and came up with strange plots to embarrass the police. Once he sat next to a prison where he knew they held some youth of his mission. Knowing how the authorities kept up the image of the country (free, democratic, respectful of human rights etc.), he pretended to be a journalist writing notes and taking pictures. In the process, he dropped all the pages on the ground so the guards could seize them. None of them could understand anything, nor could they chase him away because the prison was secret. The guards wouldn't have been able to explain why he had to leave.

Another time this Father managed to obtain permits to bring the Eucharist to his prisoners. He first had to go through endless bureaucratic procedures. Finally he went to the police chief of the prison. He took two other people, relatives of the young prisoner. The guards raised many objections. The permission was only for him, the priest. So the Father very seriously, with great pomposity, explained that the Christian religion believes in a Triune God, so the Eucharist always had to include three people. ("What? You're Catholic and you don't know these things?") The policeman let him go in along with the other two people. The ignorance of those guards was famous. They were taught only how to kill.

This situation went on for a long time. The revolution seemed imminent, but the repression was so strong that time dragged on, leaving behind dead bodies, imprisonment, and abuse. Almost all households suffered violence, kidnappings, persecutions, and searches. On the other side, the Sandinistas were preparing, and when we least expected it, they even came to us to ask if we had weapons or anything useful for the Liberation Front. Once two of them entered the house and made the cleaning girl hand over our night watchman's rifle. An elderly Sister who saw the two didn't notice anything and greeted them with a smile. Then they forced the Sister, who knew how to drive, to accompany them to another part of the city at great risk to all.

The Sisters of that house did not escape this fate. One had a brother in prison. Another had one who hid in the mountains to prepare the insurgency. Or it was a Father or a Sister, since women played a very important role in that period. Then there were the spies, who were called "ears." They were in churches, on the streets, in schools and offices. The Sandinistas were preparing to rise up, but no one, not even the best informed, knew when it would happen. The decisive year was 1979. In January, the famous opposition journalist Joaquin Chamorro, editor of the newspaper *La Prensa*, was killed. That was the straw that broke the camel's back, although five long months would pass before the insurrection. On one of my trips from Guatemala to Nicaragua, I found that one of the young Sisters of the eastern district Community was desperate. Her brother had been arrested, accused of having participated in a bank robbery. At that time, it was said, the Sandinistas were laundering money and had brigades in charge of that task. I never knew if it was true or not, but the Sister was very upset and wanted to do something to get her brother out of prison. The prisons were crammed with political prisoners and real criminals and thieves of all sorts. They were locked up in small, dark rooms, fifty or sixty huddled in terrible hygienic conditions under Managua's 40°C (104°F) heat.

The Sister was informed and was told that it would take a good lawyer to get her brother released. It would take a lot of money. At the same time, there were no lawyers who would want to defend an alleged Sandinista. The Sister, accompanied by another Sister, and sometimes by another, visited her brother almost every day to bring him something to eat because detainees were not fed. The situation became increasingly difficult. One day, during one of the visits, the brother told the Sister that they had a way to escape. Through the little window of the cell he'd seen a laborer walk past. Perched on the shoulders of a friend, he asked the guy, "Help me to escape, brother?" (In Nicaragua it's common to say "brother" as a way of trust.) The worker gave a surreptitious nod. On the day they planned to escape, his Sister and her friend were to be ready to get him with a car on a nearby street. Needless to say, the Sisters, their families, and the Congregation itself were at risk. Nobody knew anything except the other Sister and me. There was no point in moralizing at such times. She began to set things up for the terrible event. They went on the appointed day, but nothing happened. They went the next day, but nothing happened. For a week she went but saw no sign of her brother. Worried, they

Revolution in Nicaragua

returned to visit him. He sent word that it was impossible. The anxiety of the poor Sister grew day by day because detainees often disappeared and were never heard from again.

Finally, a few days later, while we were at the dinner table, we heard running in the hall entrance. It was the Sister's brother, a beautiful blond boy, tall, very thin. He had been a week without eating in order to get out through a tunnel. He was scratched and wounded on his face and arms from barbed wire. He washed quickly, went to the bathroom, and ran off. We saw him again several months after the revolution.

These events made us very anxious, tired, and worried. There was no talk of anything but the upcoming revolution. Meanwhile I was appointed Regional Superior, responsible for Central America. I was called back to Italy for one of our international meetings. It was the month of June. Just as I arrived in Rome, I was advised that the revolution had broken out. I had to return immediately because otherwise I would have been locked out. I returned immediately to Central America, going directly to Guatemala. I tried to get more precise information. They told me that they had closed all borders into Nicaragua and it was no longer possible to go there. I went to the airport to see if they had really canceled all flights. They told me that no more planes were leaving, only a military plane that was about to take off. I was carrying nothing more than my purse, a little money and a passport, but there was no time to lose. I took that last chance.

To the Ends of the Earth

The plane was nearly empty, with some soldiers and a few civilians, but I arrived in Nicaragua. The Managua airport was packed with people who wanted to leave. The only flights were military and the Red Cross. There were long queues. I tried to leave the airport, but I was prevented from leaving. All the roads were blocked. Where did I want to go? I begged, I cried, I made up a story that I had to reach my Community at all costs, but it was useless. I waited three or four hours, praying to St. Joseph, until I saw a van of the International Red Cross. I convinced the driver to take me into the city. I'd pass for a Red Cross nurse. He told me that he could only take me to the house of Monsignor Obando, Archbishop of Managua, where there was a Red Cross center.

The van had to stop at ten or twelve checkpoints before we finally reached the house of the bishop. He received me with great courtesy and entrusted me to the Sisters who ran the center. The Sisters had no space in their house, which consisted of a kitchenette and a small room with their three beds. They sent me to sleep in a nearby house. It was empty: a young lady was watching it after the owner, a rich lady, fled to the United States. That evening the good Sisters washed everything I was wearing and returned it all in the morning. Not having a suitcase and parcels was my salvation for the events that awaited me. From the bishop's house I was able to briefly phone Guatemala to tell them what had happened. All they'd known was that I'd gone to the airport and never returned. I spoke in coded language. I remained there for a week, trying in vain to reach the city of Diriamba, forty kilometers from Managua. Most of the Sisters had gathered there, though some were in the other three communities. Each was isolated from the others.

With stopgap, make-shift, ad hoc, jury-rig maneuvers, the Red Cross, and various vicissitudes, I managed to reach one of our Managua communities. The Sister who greeted me was very busy transporting injured people to the hospital. She advised me to head straight for Diriamba before it became completely isolated. She drove me in the jeep while I waved a little white flag. She left me on the street where I had to hitch a ride with anyone I met. But it was hard to get a ride because no one trusted anyone. An armor-plated car took me a long way. They were strange guys who spoke in monosyllables and scared me a little. Meanwhile it rained and I was terrified of being left on the road as soon as night fell. At 6:00 the sun went down. Darkness fell quickly. The road was broken up by very deep ruts that kept cars from passing. That's why I got dumped by the last ride. I still had five kilometers to go.

So I found myself on the side of the road, waiting for the intervention of Providence. I do not know where two soldiers of the National Guard came from. They wanted to see my documents and know where I was going. They were shocked when they realized that I wanted to continue to Diriamba. Didn't I know that I had to cross a forest that was thick with armed Sandinista guerrillas? I couldn't tell them that I had no fear of Sandinistas. They believed Sandinistas were in the thousands. In reality, every place of resistance was held by a small group that made a lot of noise, even resorting to tricks such as, for example, playing a very loud recording of the most terrible battles ever waged. The soldiers let me know that I was entering the forest at my own risk. Among the branches I glimpsed some guns. Then a young man showed up completely unarmed. I explained that I had to go on at all costs. He had me get on a scooter. He zigzagged through the forest and among the coffee plants, and put me on the right track. I clung so tight to him that he said: "Do not worry, *madre*, do not be afraid."

He dropped me off when he could no longer continue. He told me to be very careful because there were snipers in the trees. I walked for maybe three kilometers, but it seemed to take an eternity. When I got near our school, which was a very large building, I had a flash of confusion. I couldn't make it out because all the trees along the street had been cut down, and there were barricades everywhere. Arriving at the house seemed like a dream. I found it full of refugees. In the classrooms, hallways, stairs, garden, everywhere there were groups of families with their children. The Red Cross had drawn a big red cross on the roof with the hope that the air strikes would spare the center. The Sisters were trying to organize aid, to encourage people to share with each other, to lead prayer, to maintain the calm. Some of the people were friends from the neighborhood. Others we did not know. We did not know, really, who was on which side, who were Somozistas, who Sandinistas, who neutral. There were also our neighbors, rich landowners, who helped us a lot, at least to find food for all these people.

But there were also very poor people who had brought their stuff in bundles and baskets. During the bombings, chaos broke out. Everyone screamed and ran downstairs where the Sisters were staying, all the children bawling. We spent about a month like that. Food was scarce, and, because our well pump had broken, water was short. The toilets were clogged. We had to build latrines in the courtyard. We had no detergents or disinfectants, and people, afraid to go out, had dirtied every corner of the house.

We spent the nights in prayer. I was very worried, above all for the younger Sisters. If the Somozista military came along, it would be terrible. We had a suitcase ready with bare essentials in case we had to get away. Our idea was to take a nearby forest path which bordered our property. When we were tired of praying, we listened to Radio Costa Rica, which was transmitting the more truthful news, while our National Radio did nothing but assure citizens that "calm reigns throughout the country." Sometimes they warned citizens not to go out because the army was engaged in a "cleaning operation." By that they meant bombing. During those nights I learned to play chess, a lot of card games, and Chinese checkers, which older Sisters were good at. All night we Sisters had to take turns keeping watch over everybody because all kinds of things were happening. Sometimes refugees fought with each other or stole things, or you had to take in and hide fugitives. The children had a good time telling jokes and imitating General Somoza speaking English.

We heard conflicting reports. Some said the fall of the government was near. Another said the Sandinistas were losing. Among the news I heard—I never knew who had spread it—was that our superiors in Rome wanted us to take the most elderly Sisters to the airport, where the Italian ambassador had already prepared everything for their transfer to Guatemala. It was a story that bothered us a lot because the Sisters, with one exception, did not want to leave, and because it would be a major effort. I tried to find out the truth, and the ambassador in fact told me he had received a request for help to transfer the elderly nuns. I had to convince the Sisters to obey, and we prepared to face this new adventure. The poor Sisters were all octogenarians and in bad health. We had to get to the Embassy. From there the ambassador would accompany us to the airport.

We left in one of our jeeps full of worries, packages, and stuff that was rather unnecessary but that the Sisters did not want to leave behind. They all promised me that after the war they would return to Nicaragua.

The ambassador's house was on the road to Managua. To reach it, we had to go down a muddy, slippery trail through a forest. We had to stop every ten minutes when the wheels got stuck. While the Sister who was driving tried to shift into four-wheel drive, we stuffed branches and stones under the tires. The elderly murmured, between one prayer and the next, "All the fault of the Communists!" We reached the Italian Embassy, which was situated on a hill. From the terrace you could see the whole of Managua, the big lake, the volcano, the vast green areas. But now we saw only fires caused by the bombing. The ambassador had not prepared anything, nor could he tell me exactly from whom the request came, but I couldn't get into questions. What impressed me was his coolness in talking about what was going on. He was listening to classical music from a stereo and humming as he walked around the house. He had two beautiful daughters who were fuming because their parents wouldn't let them go out! The wife was very friendly with the Sisters. She made us dinner, and that night we slept at the embassy.

The next day, we took two diplomatic corps cars through the city and headed to the airport. We were stopped by soldiers ten times, and each time the ambassador explained the situation. The airport was packed with people wanting to leave Nicaragua. It was dark and without water. The toilets were filthy. We had no reservations. The ambassador got busy, got us tickets, and told us that when it was the Sisters' turn, they would travel on a Red Cross plane. And then he left. I was at the airport with five Sisters for three days, spending the night sitting up, with all sorts of problems. We had nothing to eat or drink. People who recognized us brought something to the poor old women.

To the Ends of the Earth

At night sometimes there was an alarm, but we couldn't get out. One of the Sisters broke her walker and wept with worry. I had to go find her shoes in her suitcase, which was packed with a thousand others in a storage area.

The poor nuns prayed all the time without a moan. One of them had a big phosphorescent rosary that shone at night. (Later, a young refugee designer in our high school thought about doing a comedy sketch about this.)

They finally left on the morning of the fourth day. No one was waiting at the airport in Guatemala, and the Sisters didn't know how to reach our House. I, on the way back to Diriamba, had to go to the embassy to spend a night. Then I started the adventure of traveling the forty kilometers that separated me from our House.

Meanwhile, the Sisters of Spanish nationality had left for Spain, and one from Brazil returned to her country. The rest of us remained as a group scattered in four communities. We had no news of each other. In Guatemala, they heard that all three of our Sisters in the eastern district, where the Sandinista central command was, were dead. We cried and celebrated a requiem mass, but then we found out that the Sisters had fled across the countryside as soon as they heard that the military had entered the area. Their escape was well known because they were always followed by the dog and the cat.

The uncertainty and the manipulated news made us very nervous. So people were out of their minds. The Sisters didn't know what to do or what to invent to keep people entertained. They organized focus groups, work, games, contests and prayers. I led a prayer group. The people prayed and prayed. They converted and promised to change their lives. I remember a poor woman who confessed in public that she was very glad to have her husband in prison because he was a drunk and beat her. The war had been good for her. But then a few days later her husband escaped from prison and the poor woman gave up all hope.

The killing of the American journalist Billy Stuart was decisive for the end of the revolution. The United States finally withdrew its support, and on the night of July 19, Somoza left the government and fled. Before he left, he bombed areas held by the Sandinistas by throwing barrels of TNT from airplanes! The Sandinistas won. There was a huge party. I don't know where people found the champagne that night, but they toasted, sang, and recited prayers of thanksgiving, and we did, too. But then the looting began, as did the destruction of the homes of the wealthy, who were fleeing en masse. Desolation reigned everywhere, but the war was over.

9

Sandinista Ideology
and Evangelical Commitment

A few days after the end of the war, or rather, the fall of the dictatorship—because the war never really ended—our Mother General arrived with several Sisters who had been transferred to Guatemala. They brought food and aid, and we started our life, although in a different way. Our houses were looted, especially those we'd had to abandon. They had taken everything—beds, furniture, kitchen utensils, doors and windows, electric wires, lamps. Later we recognized, in the homes of our neighbors, sheets with our initials, our chairs, our suitcases. So one day, during a homily at Mass, which generally everyone participated in, a woman who was our friend stood up and said: "I want to advise all the neighbors that the Sisters thank you very much for being so kind as to keep their things. Now, if you would like, you can bring them back. Thank you!" But nothing came back.

They had taken thirty typewriters from the school. The houses where people had taken refuge looked like chicken coops. Our gardens were destroyed. Eleven bodies were buried in the courtyard of our House, which had been the headquarters of the Sandinistas. We left it as a small cemetery. We started again from scratch. The Diriamba school, which until then had been a primary and secondary school for the upper class, became an Institute of Agronomy for rural youth. Bureaucratic issues started up and never ended. The new authorities were very kind to us, but they were struggling to manage public affairs. After a few years we were finally able to sign an agreement with the Ministry of Education. It secured some of our autonomy while the government agreed to pay our teachers. The school had to be free.

The Sandinista government initiated many reforms, starting with the literacy campaign that helped them disseminate their own ideas among the people. The local Church, which had given some support to the Sandinista revolution, did an about-face. The Vatican stood firm. It had no confidence in this new experiment, which it considered yet another communist and Marxist model.

On our part, there were many meetings with the Mother

Sandinista Ideology and Evangelical Commitment

General and the bishop, who urged us not to abandon the field of education. All the Sisters, minus those who had left Nicaragua and never returned, had to roll up their sleeves because there was so much work. The Sandinista ideology, a mix of social and Christian idealism, of communism and atheism, didn't get far with the people, but young people were more open to new ideas. Educational programs had many principles which overlapped the Gospel and which we were able to combine with our activities, but from overseas there was a fixed battle against the new government.

In Managua two very serious cultural Centers were formed that dealt with the constellation of problems relating to the Church. They were visited by people of international fame, ecclesiastical as well as secular. There were excellent theological reflections, sometimes a bit manipulated, but always of a high standard. The new socialist-Sandinista model was of interest to many scholars of politics, sociology and philosophy.

Busy as we were, rebuilding homes and schools, filling posts vacated by Sisters who had left and teachers of the old regime, resolving the daily problems of finding bread, corn, rice, beans and milk, facing endless lines to get a spare tire or a can of gas (people were saying, "We were better off when we were worse off"), we couldn't immediately get into conflicts that were being created by the new situation.

Life became very difficult, but this helped us to mature and to get closer to the life of the people and to the evangelical sense of the everyday. We Sisters met frequently to look for positive factors in the situation and to try to find people a bit of hope, given that every family had one or two people to mourn. We always finished our reflections by emphasizing our dedication to the poor, which was no longer a theoretical matter. Even if almost everyone had left Nicaragua, we would have remained in solidarity with the people who could not leave. Actually, many people, as soon as they managed to get together a little money for the trip, did leave. We were being idealistic, because we, too, in the long run, came to show signs of fatigue. Especially irksome, more than anything, were the endless gatherings that the new government called for the school, the neighborhood, the family, for the harvest of cotton or coffee. Everyone had to participate. The theme of the meetings was always the same—the revolutionary consciousness, the need to remain vigilant, the struggle against the imperialism of the United States. (A North American Sister, very open to ideas, had chosen to come to Nicaragua to work with the poor, but she left in despair after hearing so much bad about the United States!) When I phoned to find a Sister, they always replied: "She's in a meeting." Then, the same Sisters baptized the meetings "stupid," and every time I was looking for someone they answered me: "It's a stupid meeting." But the country kept on going, moving between hope, easy optimism, and awful pessimism.

During those years, many international co-operation volunteers and staff arrived in Nicaragua. They were truly the right arm of the battered economy in which the country remained. It was especially young people who moved the nation ahead.

When one left Nicaragua, one heard all sorts of things. There was talk of devastated churches, persecution, torture, and imprisonment. We tried in vain to make it clear that it was not true, that it was information exaggerated by anti-Sandinista propaganda. We were always interrupted. Here, we were told, even you are so naive as to fall into the trap. Can't you understand that there are thousands and thousands of Russians and Cubans? In a few days you won't even be able to breathe!

This problem was a constant drip that gradually penetrated people's brains, ruining the image of all those who directly or indirectly cooperated with the government. Also, we became defined as "Sandinista," and this harmed us greatly, although for us it was not a real problem. The discussions that I had to bear with nuns, priests, and friends who became enemies, were stressful. So the local Church left us to our fate. If we wanted to be the church's (and the Pope's) children. we had to repudiate anything that smacked of Sandinismo and put ourselves against it. This became part of our job. We had a lot of freedom to criticize, to express our opinion, and to stand up for our rights. The terrible polarization seemed absurd. On the contrary, we always tried to put into those stupid meetings a little Christian wisdom and real collaboration for things that were really urgent. There was talk of reconciliation, of forgiveness—the hatreds were terrible, of obedience to the Pope and respect for the bishops, but they were wasted efforts.

Meanwhile, almost immediately, the drama of the counterrevolution began. Young people were removed from the school and rushed to the borders to defend the free homeland. They left with the medal of Mother Cabrini around their necks and very often came back corpses. Sister Juanita, one of the Sisters, the school principal, had the sad task of going to identify the dismembered bodies of the poor children, our students, and then inform the mothers. There were many scenes of weeping, despair, and enormous frustration for the comfort and peace that never came. Unfortunately they could not enjoy the accomplishment of good things that were realized or have the joy of seeing the poor get educated and be able to attend university, to have a house and a better standard of living.

A few years after the revolution, I returned to Italy. The centenary of the founding of our Institute was being celebrated in Rome. Everything seemed bland and uninteresting. No one really wanted to take interest in what was happening in Nicaragua. They knew the Sandinistas were communists and prayed that everything would end soon. (We were praying for the opposite!) Here I had to put up with a lot of discussion; the analyses which were made were very superficial, even if there was some truth. I felt a terrible annoyance and could not wait to return. Once, going to New York, I happened to arrive just before the American presidential elections. The Sisters of the Community were speaking so highly of Reagan that I sensed that they would vote for him. Of course out of respect I could not get into the issue. The next day, when I learned that Reagan had been re-elected, an unspeakable sadness hit me. The Sisters noticed it. I explained my disappointment. Poor things, they said that if they had known those things beforehand, they would not have voted for Reagan, but I did not believe it. The pressure against Communism was an infallible weapon. Traveling in Argentina was even worse. The country was under a total military regime and they had very clear ideas about the fact that we were Marxists-Leninists, while on the other hand their president went to Mass every Sunday, had I not seen it in photographs?

Despite all, we never lost hope. In Central America, life went on among thousands of difficulties, but we organized a trip to the Atlantic coast, attempting to retrace the path taken by Mother Cabrini in 1892. It was a magnificent trip! We followed the Rio Escondido, stopping at some beautiful places, in a motor-boat much safer than the barges used by Mother Cabrini, although we experienced a storm and a certain fear. The little boat took channels that were like tunnels of palm trees and beautiful plants with all kinds of orchids hanging down in bunches. We left a picture of Mother Cabrini in a little church in a splendid village where there were no roads; the post-built houses were separated by lawns. The houses were open, and people gathered in the evening in the village center to decide things of common interest. Each house had a section of the river where they could wash, hang out laundry, get water, and relax. They were Misquitos, the same people Mother Cabrini had met.

The Sisters were very much a part of the community, and I, perhaps, committed an innocent sin. The country was split in two; whatever you did to be closer to the other side, there was always some new conflict that destroyed the fragile work of the community. Even among the poor there were people who hated the Sandinistas. The so-called "Contras" worked from outside to create disturbances and availed themselves of the international press. One day when I was in the house of some Fathers, an Italian journalist was interviewing people for an article in a Catholic newspaper. When he saw me, he wanted to ask a few questions; one of the Fathers (the Superior), hearing my views, interrupted the interview and, almost shouting, began to contradict me and explain to the journalist that what I said were all fables, that they, the Fathers, had for years done everything that I had said the Sandinistas were doing. Any opinion of mine was useless. The reporter listened to the Father, and the article came out completely manipulated by the holy priest. A few years later, I wrote a fiery letter to the editor. I do not know if they have it on file.

The Holy Father's visit to Nicaragua demonstrated the mismanagement of things. The evening before his arrival lots of incidents were created to demonstrate to the Pope that in Nicaragua there was religious persecution.

Sandinista Ideology and Evangelical Commitment

My personal position was in the balance, especially for the fact that I was vice president of the Conference of Religious of Nicaragua, which was not well regarded by the local Church because they were accused of being Sandinistas. The president, Father Juan Ramon Moreno, a Jesuit, a great religious man, balanced and serene, did everything to keep the conference out of the conflicts with the local Church. He worked quietly, but the opposition forces spread the word, alleging that our behavior only served to worsen the situation. One day a handful of people, including a priest and a nun, arrived in Nicaragua, sent by no one knew whom. They wanted to know how things were going in Nicaragua and what the religious were doing. They wanted to come and visit us. We very politely explained to them what was happening. Later we learned that these people had sent "Rome" a rather negative report on the Conference of Religious.

It was a real shock. I even complained to the embassy. But I had to be very careful. The repression in Guatemala had reached its worst. We lost friends who were priests and young people of the parish youth group. Many foreigners were deported and the religious who left were not allowed to return. One famous incident was the kidnapping of a priest who'd been very active in the fight against repression. After a few weeks, they had him appear on television. He asked forgiveness for having spread Liberation Theology, which he said had been the cause of so many victims of communism. He spoke for more than three hours, and every day they rebroadcast a piece of that dramatic speech. The priest was never heard from again.

We had to take many precautions. I could only recommend that the Sisters be careful, but then we had to trust in God. We were very much involved with the martyrdoms in Guatemala. Persecuted people from various areas of Central America, especially El Salvador and Guatemala, were arriving in Nicaragua. The death of so many priests and religious friends often brought us together in prayer. Our conference president, Father Ramon, celebrated the Eucharist and explained how those martyrs would be the seed of Central American liberation. Some years later, Father Ramon was killed along with four other priests in El Salvador.

In early 1983 our General Superior came to visit. Between what was heard in Rome and what was said in the United States, she wanted to see for herself. She was very reserved and would not listen to much from us. I had to accompany her to see the cardinal, who said that among us there were Sandinistas and he could prove it with a tape that was recorded in which you could hear the voice of one of our Sisters. I was left shocked, and expecting a reaction from the General Superior, who, to the contrary, was very grave.

When we left the meeting I made negative comments about the meeting. How had it hapened? Did the Cardinal have spies? The Mother General left Nicaragua very annoyed. She told me not to take up any more initiatives. At the time I didn't understand what she meant.

A few months later, she wrote me a letter, in which she said I was suspended from my duties because I was very tired. I was to be transferred. I was, in fact, tired and, indeed, after her departure I wrote that I did not like her behavior during the visit and that I, tired as I was, did not receive any support from her, and so on. Upon learning of my transfer, the Sisters felt very bad, as did I. In my naiveté, I didn't understand too well what lay beneath my transfer. This delay in understanding negative things about myself has always been my salvation. In any case, I packed up and was sent to Argentina " to rest."

I went to Colombia, where members of the Conference of Latin American Religious wanted to know what had happened. They had wanted me to accept the assignment in Nicaragua. They had similar problems, problems that lasted for years.

When I found myself alone at the airport in Bogotá with my two suitcases in the middle of winter in South America, after the heat of Nicaragua, I understood that this was an important parenthesis in my life, that there was nothing to cry about, or to despair about, nor to demand an explanation from anyone, it was only to make a choice, one of many in my life: to look forward!

10

The Matiguás Mission—Successes and Failures

Before concluding my parenthesis in Central America, I want to talk about Matiguás, not because it was the most important mission I've lived through or known, but because for me it has a symbolic function.

From that experience, in fact, we can observe, on a small scale, a summary of what a mission can be: hopes and expectations, small satisfactions and great disappointments, irreconcilable conflicts, broad variety of ways of thinking, closures and openings, good and evil, ambiguity and painful certainties, failures.

Matiguás is a small town located in the central region of the north of Nicaragua. The Pan-American Highway that runs through all the Central American countries, from northern end in Mexico down to the southern end in Argentina, reaches about three hundred kilometers from Managua to a city named Boaco. Here you leave the Pan-American Highway and proceed inland for about 75 kilometers. A good driver could not do this last stretch in less than three hours, the road being so bumpy and broken up. It should be considered a big trail more than a road. It took me—never an adept driver—at least four hours.

The idea of opening a mission in that area was born from the change in missionary vision that had been developing since the Medellin Conference of Latin American bishops in 1965. On that occasion the bishops, making a serious analysis of the situation in Latin America, denounced the great social and economic imbalances that plagued the continent. They pointed out that the Church, as well as its religious life, cooperated, perhaps unknowingly, with the unbalanced situation and the gap between rich and poor. In a certain way, they had been fostering and strengthening the unjust system. Among other things, they also pointed out that most of the convents and religious works were located in large urban centers and served, for the most part, the wealthy class. The poor, already marginalized by the political powers and the military dictatorships, were also marginalized by the Church and the religious. Following this denunciation, there were big changes. Many religious institutes abandoned the great colleges to go to the outskirts of cities or rural areas.

The Matiguas Mission—Successes and Failures

When I arrived in Nicaragua in 1974, this debate had already moved ahead, although support was, in general, from the foreign religious or indigenous young people. In our congregation it was precisely the younger Sisters, especially those native to the region, who spoke up for the need to establish new foundations in the urban periphery and in the poorest areas of the country. For some time Sister Francesca, a Sister from Argentina, was said to be particularly expert in these issues. In fact, she had already set up, for better or worse, a new Cabrini operation on the outskirts of Managua.

Before the Sandinista revolution, the regional superior, Sister Victoria del Solar, had done all the preliminaries to open a new mission in the rural area of Matiguás. The Sisters were to work with the Fathers of a well-known order. We had already prepared to go to the area during the summer holidays, knowing all the details.

I was particularly excited about the news. I saw in it, finally, a concrete place in which to apply all the new ideas about mission that were being internalized by the novices I was responsible for.

Sister Francesca herself, with an inseparable friend, Father Florián, joined us for the first time to learn about the famous mission. Although he traveled in a comfortable, air-conditioned Toyota, that first trip seemed unending. Leaving the main road, the trail that led to Matiguás, just 75 kilometers, was an endless khaki snake, all ups and downs, curves with dangerous chasms on one side and large holes that sometimes were filled with dirt and with the least rain became veritable quagmires of mud where the wheel of any vehicle bogged down. That was during the rainy season, from May to October. During the dry season the road was a cloud of dust and potholes that put a strain on the wheels, clutch and brakes.

Father Florián was a North American Capuchin, a very good Father, generous and simple, idealistic and with a bit of a messianic complex as, indeed, Sister Francesca had. Both were elected president and secretary, respectively, of the Conference of Religious of Nicaragua, which combined the religious congregations of men and women, though generally it was not regarded well by the bishops. The Conference people had been all over Nicaragua, convening the religious and presenting their new course of religious life. They were appreciated for their ideas and their good will but, as always happens in these cases, there were those who spoke well of them, and those who couldn't stand them. But they continued to unabashedly believe that they were bearers of new ideas. Despite criticism, they went on undeterred.

During the trip they had us do a "theological reflection," as they called it. As the Father drove, Sister Francesca read a passage of Scripture or the latest book of CLAR, which had just came out. Then there was a long silence and finally we made various comments. That day the comment was more or less along the style of the mission that was necessary for our time and for

The Matiguas Mission—Successes and Failures

the difficulties that we would encounter in Matiguás, because the Fathers we had to work with were somewhat traditionalist. We exchanged knowing looks with Sister Victoria. The looks were a little because of the way Sister Francesca was carrying on the conversation, as if before an assembly of religious, seconded in everything by Father Florián; and a little because, coming to the new mission and talking with the Fathers, we already imagined where we were going to end up. The conversation lasted a few hours until we decided to stop in the shade of a beautiful mango tree to have a snack. As a good American, Father Florián had brought fresh bread, cheese and salami (which is extremely rare in Nicaragua), some candy, fruit and Coca-Cola. After the break the journey continued through my sighs because I had the impression that we would never arrive.

When we arrived at our destination, we took a look through the town. It was decidedly ugly. The road descended to a ravine which in winter was filled with water, and then resumed until we came to a perpendicular crossroad, forming a huge T. Here and there along the street were little, battered houses painted with gaudy colors. This sense of ugliness gave an immediate bad impression. I continued to cultivate the ideal of a mission located among poor and marginalized people, but I had never come to terms with the question of aesthetics.

It took us a long time to find the Fathers. Some people gave us directions one way, others gave directions another way. We finally managed to understand that the only person who was truly informed was a Señora Chilita, who served as parish secretary. She was a spinster belonging to one of the area's few rich families, people we would have to deal with.

When we managed to see one of the Fathers, we realized the disorganization and the carelessness with which they treated the arrival of the Sisters and, even more, the very little interest they had to talk about pastoral methods and new missionary guidelines. We blamed the absence of the other priest, and that evening there was no talk of anything but the needs of the people, who were mostly spread all over the surrounding mountains, while the Fathers did nothing but talk about the squalid conditions in which the people had been found when they had arrived fifty years earlier. We returned to Managua very late and due to our exhaustion had little desire to make comments.

Nonetheless, shortly thereafter, even though there was no House for the Sisters, the mission opened. The Sisters had to stay in a room in the Father's house. The Sisters were supposed to take care of the elementary, middle and high schools, the medical dispensary, and all parish operations. There were three designated Sisters, including a novice who was to have her first apostolic experience.

At first they tried to overcome the endless difficulties of getting settled into the community one day at a time with a little humorous spirit, although the three Sisters—a senior who was the Superior, and two young ones—had to make real efforts to

The Matiguas Mission—Successes and Failures

curb their critical sense. The first serious challenge was having to live in one room in the house of the Fathers, without schedules, without any organization or perspective. The only good thing was that the Sisters could pray every morning with the Fathers and celebrate the Eucharist. The Sisters immediately sought another accommodation. It was very difficult. The few decent houses were occupied by the owners. To build their house the Sisters would have to wait several more months. Finally, one of the Fathers, Father Luigi, a young Italian friar, persuaded a wealthy landowner who owned a house in town that was used as a warehouse, to let the nuns live there for a while. It was a large room with hollow brick walls from which came tremendous dust. The windows were up near the roof, perhaps to keep out thieves. The Sisters made the best of it, closing some parts of the walls and putting up some divisions to make some of the rooms a little more private. In the back they organized a kitchen and a kind of bath.

As the Sisters became conscious of the environment, they came to understand the many differences of missionary approach and culture, not to mention educational methodology, which almost did not exist.

The Fathers lived under those conditions with great spirit of sacrifice and generosity, but they did not realize how dramatic were these conditions which caused for the Sisters, as educators and as women, great discomfort, habituated as they were to our schools, which, though poor, were always very neat and clean.

To the Ends of the Earth

The primary school was held in three shifts: morning, afternoon, and evening. In the evening lessons were given for middle and secondary school. After every class, the students had a few minutes to clean up the classroom. They had to do so without water, brooms or cleaning materials, with the dust coming in non-stop from windows. The windows were just louvered shutters, which trapped a stifling heat. There were no floors, just the earth that was pressed firm with water, though the water couldn't be overdone or it turned to chalky mud. To quench their thirst, the children had to take water from bins of rainwater.

The Fathers had certainly done wonders to get permits from the Ministry of Education to manage the school, which was a dream for hundreds of illiterate children. The poor Fathers even had the courage to go to the university with a group of young people who came to Managua every Saturday morning (starting at three a.m.) and returned at midnight. The Sisters, however, were uneasy with the poor quality of the teachers (almost none of them had a diploma), and with the total lack of discipline, hygiene, programs and responsibilities. The superiors of the order could hardly wait for the Fathers to hand over responsibility for the school and dedicate themselves only to evangelization.

Evangelization at that time consisted of what the Sisters called "sacramentalism." Here, too, the Fathers were heroes, but catechesis, training, and preparation for the sacraments

The Matiguas Mission—Successes and Failures

were rather precarious. In town they celebrated the liturgy and traditional festivals. In the rural and mountainous areas, the Fathers went once a year, after days and days of walking on horseback or on foot, stopping where there was a group of houses. There, hundreds of people gathered for the only confession and Mass of the year or for baptisms, weddings and funerals. All was done in great haste and without any preparation. Sometimes the Sisters accompanied a Father and tried to lend a little organization. It was almost impossible, however, because in addition to all that, they had to carry crates of medicine. In fact many people came to be treated more in body than in spirit. Poor Father Luigi, when he came back from those missions, was just skin and bones. His robe hung down from his shoulders, and he screamed like a neurasthenic because he believed that people were stubborn, and he couldn't think calmly. Between animals and lice, he had slept badly for months, so of course he was exhausted.

The Sisters were trying to establish a dialogue on pastoral method, but there were always discussions, so that the old Superior begged the two young Sisters to keep quiet so as not to lose charity and respect. I remember once I was in a small town where I had to get the bishop to administer the sacrament of confirmation. The Fathers took advantage of this to do baptisms, bless weddings, first communions etc. One of our Sisters was trying to write a long list of faithful who were to receive a sacrament. They were so many that at one point

I heard the Sister say: "Baptism, thirty, confirmation, fifty," and so on. It was the number of people who were to be given the sacraments, but the impression was that they were selling sacraments. I intervened and said, "What are you doing?" She had no idea what I meant!

Whenever I went to Matiguás, all I did was listen to complaints. The young novices were dismayed, but at the same time, being native to Nicaragua, they felt entitled to make it clear to the Fathers, both of whom were Italian, that their method was wrong, that though they sacrificed a lot, they treated people as if they were passive and ignorant, and they did nothing to elevate their human quality.

The other Father, Father Stefano, who was more adult, was a strange man though very dedicated. He had worked hard to try to build healthcare facilities and schools. He ran the dispensary. He probably had some medical knowledge, but he confused fat women with pregnant and passed out medicines, syrups, pills and such with great liberty, horrifying the Sister who replaced him. People were very appreciative of the medicines the Father gave them. But there were disagreements over even this. The Sister let the doctors who came around once a week make the decisions, while the Father believed it was a serious lack of charity to send away the poor people who had just walked two hundred kilometers to get there, only to be told to return the following Saturday.

Father Stefano was not open to change, though he pretended

The Matiguas Mission—Successes and Failures

to listen. During Mass, he gave long sermons and did not realize that most of the people were sleeping, especially in the evening when there was no light and the church was lit by only a dim candle. He spoke a Spanish soaked with Italian words, mixing themes of catechism with tales of what had happened in the mission or happened to him as a child or told some anecdote about the saints, and no one understood anything. People told him they did not understand, but he didn't change. Once I traveled with him from Matiguás to Managua. Nearly seven hours of travel. He talked the whole time without giving me the slightest chance to speak.

The conflict between the mentality of the Fathers and the methods of the Sisters became always more acute, although in day-to-day life, conflict faded before the urgent needs that they constantly had to deal with—sudden deaths, sick persons to be accompanied to the hospital, family quarrels (the people were particularly quarrelsome), sudden decisions because, for example, a priest didn't arrive and we had to entertain people in church with rosaries and stations of the cross. And then there was the school, which was really the thorn in the side of the mission.

This went on for a while until, finally, the Sisters were able to have their home. It was on the other side of town, near the church of St. Joseph. It was built according to more feminine criteria, such as bathrooms, although there was no water, though later the Sisters dug a well. In the land surrounding the house they planted flowers, fruit, and a vegetable garden. Now, when we went to visit the Sisters, we felt more relaxed in the familial atmosphere. They could pray in the chapel, and we could talk about our lives and our problems. The garden was a real solution. The town was not organized. They went weeks without finding potatoes, carrots or a sprig of parsley, which was strange in a place where fenceposts bore flowers within a month. It was especially difficult during the rainy season, when the town could be isolated for months due to the poor condition of the roads. Most necessities, such as cooking gas, candles, drinking water, oil, and sugar had to be brought from Managua.

In Matiguás you had to protect against parasites, malaria, dysentery. You had to sleep with large mosquito nets to avoid being eaten to death by mosquitoes and other creatures, but in the new house, the Sisters kept everything under control. One big problem remained—the logistical situation of the school. To reach it, the Sisters had to cross the town, make a long descent to the ravine, and then make a strenuous climb up to the church, school and dispensary. We bought a jeep. It was a great help in reaching the nearby rural and impassable areas. But every two weeks we had to replace the tires, which got punctured continuously, and clean the engine, and change the oil, and check the steering and the brakes. Often the Sisters got stranded. As for the school, it was urgent to come up with new solutions, but we had to have the approval of the Fathers and of those who had "the power behind the throne," such

The Matiguás Mission—Successes and Failures

as the famous lady Chilita. Such people are very common in missions, and even if they're a huge nuisance, they take on certain responsibilities. Without them, we could not go on, but their control was a real punishment from God. But with their collaboration, Father Luigi managed to make progress. He always went with lead feet because the Fathers had to weigh every change we made, implying a lack of self-sacrifice on our part.

The early years of the Matiguás mission coincided with the harsh repression of the Somoza dictatorship that was by now winding down. The landowners of the area, owners of hundreds of hectares of land partially cultivated with corn, cotton or pasture and partly uncultivated, traveled armed to the teeth for fear of the Sandinista guerrillas who were hiding in the mountains preparing the revolution.

For this reason, the Fathers did not want to hear about a new style of pastoral or liberation work, because everything had to be interpreted in a political sense.

By the end of the third year that we were in Matiguás, our strength was exhausted from having to carry out a huge job under terribly precarious conditions. This fatigue was taken by some as evidence of our inability to hold up, but it was obvious that the Sisters spent a lot of energy to make things work, and when they weren't there, nobody was interested in making those things work. But this could not be easily shown, nor was it a matter of rattling off all the troubles put upon the poor Sisters. Often they lacked teachers in the school, so the Sisters had to make up for hours and hours of classes, from first grade through high school. For that reason we decided, after advising the Fathers and the Provincial Superior, to decrease our commitment. The following year we did not open the high school, which there was called a *bachillerato*. We kept only the elementary school and middle school. There were complaints to no end, but the conditions to continue did not exist. We also advised the local board of education that, given the school's shortcomings, the upper classes would not be continued.

One evening a few months after the beginning of the school year, after the afternoon Mass, we saw outside the school a long line of young people and adults who usually had attended the *bachillerato*. We asked what they wanted. They said that they were waiting for the school to reopen. We explained that there would be no more classes because there were no teachers, programs, or rooms. But they stood there waiting in rain that fell in torrents. The next night the same thing happened, and it continued throughout the week. They were mostly young men in their twenties and thirties, all farmers, already married, perhaps already divorced. Certainly their dreams had been interrupted. When they returned home, the Sisters wept and were compelled to reopen the higher courses.

The efforts to bring order to the situation (records, programs, report cards, certificates, schedules of students who were doing three years in one, etc.) and the long trips to and long waits at

The Matiguas Mission—Successes and Failures

the Ministry of Education were beyond description. The Sisters continued to seek solutions and money to fund the courses, but the students' progress was poor. We didn't know how to get out of this impasse.

One day our General Superior came to visit us. She wanted to see the new mission. It was a memorable visit. The Fathers welcomed her with great courtesy. They explained to the people that this was the first General Superior to come to Matiguás, and at Mass they praised the Sisters. The General Superior spoke to the people, and I translated. The following day the Fathers invited us all to dinner. For the occasion they had also invited their Superior, and other Fathers. We all sat at the table. There were ten Fathers and six or seven Sisters. Señora Chilita served the Superior first and then one by one the Fathers. When the dishes arrived on our side they were completely empty or with some miserable remnant. The thing was so grotesque that we did not know whether to laugh or cry. Until the end of the meal, no one noticed (or they pretended not to notice) that we weren't eating. Our spirit of humor saved us, but I was terribly ashamed.

The Mother General was quivering with desire to speak to the Fathers about the situation at the school she had visited. She, who had been rector of Cabrini College in Radnor, Pennsylvania, in the United States, a little jewel of the Cabrinis, was shocked by the conditions of our school. But it was impossible; the Fathers ignored her and she went away extremely frustrated.

We decided to build ourselves a new school. The Mother

TO THE ENDS OF THE EARTH

General would finance it.

We began to look for a suitable plot of land. The Fathers were willing to give us land that had been donated to them, which was far enough away from the village. It had belonged to a wealthy family in the town. I think it was the Reyes family. They owned three-quarters of the surrounding land. The Sisters, when they saw the awkward position of the land, didn't dare to speak: "Don't look a gift horse in the mouth." I, however, didn't resign myself.

I remember that one day, looking at the beautiful land that stretched right across the street from our new house, I said: "This is right for our new school." And I prayed to St. Joseph that he make the acquisition possible. I talked of it to the Sisters, who looked at me dumbfounded. Wasn't the idea absurd?

I however marveled that such strange ideas would come only to me. But we talked to Father Luigi. He was a difficult man to approach, but he was the only one who had certain possibilities in hand. A few days later we learned that the owner of the land was willing to trade it for another, exactly the one the Fathers had received as a donation. It didn't seem real. I myself would take care of the matter, which was quite intricate. But in difficult countries like that, you can get intricate things done more easily because of the absolute lack of legal structures. I made many trips to Matagalpa, a city to the north where the notary was. After solving various problems I managed to have the donated land signed over. The notary said it could not be

The Matiguas Mission—Successes and Failures

registered before a certain time, but the land was ours!

Meanwhile, however, the political situation was pressing in from all sides. The Sandinista revolution broke out. The Sisters found themselves in the eye of the storm because Matiguás was terribly hostile to new ideas. The landowners fled. Some were brutally killed, their homes looted and destroyed. Others hid in the mountains to prepare the counter-revolution. There was no lack of people saying that the Sisters were Sandinista, only because we allowed ourselves to defend the most basic rights of the weakest.

Immediately after the revolution, when we were able to travel again, we again took up discussion of the construction of the new school for the poor. The funding came to us from abroad, from our General Superior, and I started the adventure of building the school.

I got to know the way to Matiguás and back like the back of my hand. The design and execution of the project proved to be complicated because of the marshy land and the chalky earth. What looked like a beautiful valley wasn't actually flat. The poor builder, given his lack of resources, went crazy. We had to have workers come in from Managua because we knew them better. Construction material had to come from far away—everything: iron, sand, cement, stone, bricks. We had to hurry to procure it because with the new economy there soon arrived shortages, especially iron and cement. As we bought materials, we had to store them in large, well guarded makeshift sheds because everything got stolen from us. Sometimes the guards themselves were the thieves. Workers we had contracted worked for a week but then tired of coming from so far away and never returned. Other times they got drunk and created problems, flirting with the local women. We had to lay them off. We started construction with all kinds of difficulties, especially the rain that filled the foundation we'd just dug with water and mud. It was strange to see the workers empty ditches with little containers the size of a cup.

It was the better season that came to our rescue. Meanwhile, our budget not only doubled but tripled. Inflation was a tragedy. Nobody wanted to deal in the local currency, only in dollars. We began the adventure of changing money on the black market because the banks wouldn't do it. The new system had to tolerate the very numerous houses of exchange.

I do not know who gave me so much talent for construction and so much grit. I went down dusty roads in truckloads of cement to make sure dozens of bags didn't disappear, or of bricks or iron. Often I got home so tired that I only wanted to take a shower and go to bed. But as soon as I arrived I had to watch those who unloaded the truck, and, along with another Sister, to inspect the work and answer a thousand questions. The engineer we had contracted showed up only once! Fortunately we had a good builder.

I think my strength to go forward came from the dream of seeing the new school. Often I found myself making plans and

THE MATIGUAS MISSION—SUCCESSES AND FAILURES

designs. I dreamed of paths covered with grass, beds full of flowers, an orchard adjoining the backyard, the garden. The classrooms were designed with double wooden ceilings because, generally, the ceilings of schools were only sheet metal, which became suffocating in the sun. When you were inside, you passed out from the heat. I remember little children coming to school with washcloths in their hands to wipe up their sweat.

Finally we managed to complete the construction and to start the new school year in the new school! We had to fence it all in because yet another problem had arisen. The sons of the richer people who had survived the war believed that the school was a Sandinista project. They began a war against all Sandinista structures. They torched new health centers and new small schools that had been built for rural people. Our school really had nothing to do with the Sandinistas although the Sisters were trying to obtain payment of teachers from the new government. We had signed an agreement for that payment for our other schools in Nicaragua. The Sandinista government said it would finance only if the school had a technical program. Our new Superior, who went to Matiguás, believed that in an area of peasants, a classic *bachillerato* was absurd.

This shift in scholastic perspective was not well accepted by the people in Matiguás, even if the basic curriculum prepared them for access to other branches of education. It was impressive that the new type of school was rejected not only by the rich but by the poor. In short, everyone wanted to have the chance to become doctors and lawyers, although ninety percent of the people not only never finished the courses but ended up working the land. A fatal obstructionism began. It took the form of vandalism of the new school—to the tears of the poor Sisters—a boycott of the professors, who incited students to revolt and miss school, and people's indifference. People became more and more hostile and were almost unable to look toward the future with any hope. The real poor, less enslaved by the old thought patterns, tried to work together, but they had to endure, along with the Sisters, a cold war that was unleashed every time anyone proposed something new. On the other hand, Sandinista programs pushed certain activities such as the harvesting of cotton and coffee (I did it too!), military exercises, and so on.

The political situation, therefore, brought out once again the difference in opinion and pastoral thought of the Fathers. While acknowledging that the previous dictatorship had caused the bloody revolution, they now took reactionary positions, defending the "poor landowners" who had retreated to Miami to prepare the counteroffensive, boycotting the new laws.

The position of the Sisters became critical. As an educational system, we inevitably had to adopt the programs of the ministry. Meanwhile, the conflict with the old landowners worsened into a new guerrilla war. At school we had to try to be neutral and use plenty of wisdom in the rain of endless slander. The "Contra" counterrevolution broke out, and Matiguás became the center

The Matiguas Mission—Successes and Failures

of the counterrevolutionary organization. Then the government came in with the military. The mountains were full of Contras, those who wanted to drive the Sandinistas from power. No night passed without dozens of wounded or dead at the town's little hospital.

Before the revolution, the hospital was a small, shabby, unkempt health center. People were terrified of ending up in there, because it was said that only the dead came out. Patients were treated badly, there was almost never a doctor, and nurses did not exist or did what they felt like doing. After the revolution, the Sandinistas restructured and established new health centers and new schools. The Matiguás hospital quickly became more efficient because it was in a hotspot. But the reason for its efficiency was also due to two fundamental factors: the arrival of international cooperation doctors and health technicians, who were very efficient in post-revolutionary Nicaragua, and the work of one of our Sisters, who, having finished her nursing studies, was obliged to do two years of community service. She opted to do it in Matiguás because our Community was there. For certain reasons I'll call her Sister Marcella.

Sister Marcella, a Spanish woman in her forties, was very active, friendly and generous. She was in the hospital day and night, and she immediately changed the style and the reputation of the center. She rehabilitated the center with cleanliness, order, schedules, hospitality, and caring for people, and with the help of foreign doctors, among them Italians, Belgians,

Mexicans, and Argentines. Sister Marcella applied herself to obtaining government aid and personnel. She also sought aid from international organizations, which were particularly generous with revolutionary Nicaragua. She developed courses in prevention and hygiene. She went to nearby rural areas to open other centers despite the dangerous presence of Contras. She maintained a climate of collaboration and serenity. The few times she was home at night, she was called out for the arrival of wounded and dead. Sister Marcella spent long hours reassembling dead bodies which had to be turned over to the devastated families who came to get them.

This situation did not improve our relations with the people, the town, and the Fathers. It made them worse. Even the Fathers kept their distance from us. We were at the service of the Sandinistas!

Sister Marcella was a very sensitive person but not one to analyze facts. Perhaps she had little vocational identity. Perhaps she had some conflict within herself that she suppressed. She let herself get taken away by her work. With much simplicity, she let herself be fascinated by military uniforms, though nothing scandalous happened. When I went to Matiguás I was increasingly puzzled by the involvement of Sister Marcella with the situation. Her natural goodness and generosity caused her to overwork, to stay in the hospital even when not strictly necessary. With her it was difficult to establish a critical dialogue because everything was justified by the situation of constant emergency.

The Matiguas Mission—Successes and Failures

The local Mother Superior never understood my concerns. She indulged Sister Marcella in everything by citing certain clichés—the option for the poor, ends justify the means, etc. A Sister dedicated to her work to the point of heroism wasn't something to be admired. But I perceived in Sister Marcella a gradual emptying of objective judgment and a willful departure from the religious Community. She felt herself at the service of the poor. Was it possible no one in the Congregation could understand that?

We tried to move the Sister to another post, but it seemed a a shame to do so. In short, things went ahead as before. A few years later, when I was no longer in Nicaragua, Sister Marcella asked to leave the Congregation. The reasons she gave was a lack of understanding by her superiors, including me. Then, having received the rescript from the Holy See, she married a Sandinista commander, from whom she separated shortly thereafter.

The case of Sister Marcella was not the only cause of my apprehension. Other young Sisters were so involved in the local and national conflict that it seemed impossible to get them to step back. Sister Angelica, for example, got so carried away in her commitment to the people that she put them ahead of all other commitments, including religious ones. When we transferred her, she left the Congregation.

Local conflicts and difficulties were so bad that we were forced to change the Sisters of the Community several times.

To the Ends of the Earth

Foreigners headed to our Community a little for the welcome and the family spirit, a little for the natural need for friendship in a country that offered nothing but problems. This fact generated many misunderstandings. These foreigners were of all kinds: communists, anarchists, atheists, conscientious objectors dodging military servicy, technicians, and activists. Sometimes they were very good. Sometimes they were real slackers. But the Sisters' house was seen as a meeting place for these good-for-nothings. In fact these people were going there to eat better and for a change of scenery. They at least appreciated us.

Despite everything, the mission went ahead. The school, protected by the determination of the Missionary Sisters, was a true oasis. The flowers were growing. The garden produced. We had a chicken coop. The orchard yielded its first fruits. Our first students graduated. The covert war, however, did not let up.

In my heart a question often emerged: Why don't people love us?

I remember one day I was traveling alone to Managua, driving at a speed of about fifty or sixty kilometers per hour because of the increasingly disastrous conditions of the road. I let myself slip into a long reflection. I often thought at length while driving: two, three, four hours. We'd been on that mission for almost ten years. We'd spared no sacrifices, prayers, ideas, money, initiatives, or people. We faced all kinds of difficulties. We had defended the poor before the deadly attacks of the dictatorship, then defended them from the pressures of the

The Matiguas Mission—Successes and Failures

Sandinistas. We even defended them from pastorally oppressive master-Fathers by trying to use a new style based on invitation, persuasion, and active participation. We had given the people a real school that was free, clean, and efficient, with programs and real content. We made all our energy, home, and resources available. We had not distinguished between rich and poor even when our tendency was towards the poor, and we had tried to mediate the differences, to heal the broken, to participate in the life of the people without expecting anything in return. We had gained nothing and, in fact, we had given and almost lost the best Sisters, Sisters who had all paid the price of that experience. We thought that we had loved these headstrong, indifferent, stubborn, difficult people. But why were we not loved?

I could not find an answer. I observed that, despite everything, the Fathers were loved, or so it seemed to me. Maybe their method was the best, even though for us it was pure sacramentalism. Just distribute sacraments, shout, give people what they asked for, hold processions in the street, and be left in peace? So, what do we do wrong?

My reflection was shared by all the Sisters. Despite all the limitations, we really did our best. Those people were a symbol for us—the symbol of that which does not want change. Politics, poverty, religion, the bleak life they led, the deaths for unjust reasons that people supported—these things had nothing to do with the reasons for our failure. The real point of the conflict was a mindset that was overly crystallized. It determined all behavior. It waged war in order to resist any hint of change. For whatever reasons, therefore, even an oppressed, miserable, meaningless life without a future is preferable to the risk of the slightest change. This was my conclusion.

But then...was it all useless?

Some facts came to mind that enlightened the darkness of my reflection a little.

One day, during one of my visits to Matiguás, I found in our Sisters' Community a young girl of fifteen. Her name was Consuela.

Sister Felicia, the first Superior of the Community, had gone to a little village close to a mission. There she met the girl. She was moved to pity by her story, so she brought her to the convent. The girl was really a mountain flower. Tall and slender, perfect body, beautiful green eyes, her skin a golden tan. Orphaned of both parents, she lived with her grandmother in the mountains in a completely isolated area. There she dug in the garden all day, took care of the animals, washed and cooked without a minute of rest. Her only dream was to someday be able to study. Her brother, older than her, promised that one day he would help her. But she found out, quite by chance and to her surprise, that the grandmother had promised to marry her off to a farmer thirty years older than her. The next morning, terrified, she got up at three o'clock and ran away from home. By midday she arrived, out of breath, at the nearest little

The Matiguas Mission—Successes and Failures

town. Tired and hungry, she asked a woman to take her into her house. She said she would do anything to be able to study, at least in the evening. The woman welcomed her and promised to let her study. But she had to wash the laundry that the woman was doing for several families. Consuela got up at three in the morning, loaded into a big basket more laundry than she could carry, and went to the river to wash until late morning. Then laid the clothes out to dry, then took them back home. She did this maybe three or four times a day. In the evening—she was enrolled in evening school, —she attended classes. When she met the Sister, she told her that she was sick of that life, that the lady exploited her excessively, and that she wanted to become a Sister because she feared that her grandmother was going to take her back. In pity Sister Felicia could not resist. She brought the girl home.

The younger Sisters of the Community complained a lot. They felt it was wrong that the girl lived in the Community while she still had to figure out what the religious life was. Of course, Sister Felicia didn't see the girl's motivation as sufficient reason, but she was heartbroken by the girl's story, which she had told with great innocence and humility. When I arrived and spoke with the girl, I let myself get involved. She was willing to do anything, and she understood very well that to become a woman religious, one had to go through a long discernment. I urged her to get a job and live an independent life while continuing to study. But there was nothing to be done. She wanted to be with

141

us. We told her it would be a provisional stay while we looked for a solution more suitable for her (Consuela stayed with us fifteen years). She started to go to school. She attended the first elementary courses in the morning, others in the afternoon, and in the evening she took the more advanced courses. She studied night and day. Though we tried to get her to slow down, she wouldn't change her mind, even though she was no genius and often got tired. She managed to pass elementary school. The following year she got her high school diploma. Then she went on to the bachillerato and studied to be a nurse. She performed social service in rural areas and war zones, and she remained chaste, which is very unusual in those circumstances. For many years she worked at a medical dispensary in Guatemala and enrolled in the university for a degree in psychology. She never became either a Sister or a lay missionary. Still, she was a symbol of success, almost an antidote to other examples that were much less edifying.

Another fact entered the new light of my thoughts: Father Luigi. We had known him as a closed and intransigent person, authoritarian and ready to scold, traditional and a slave to tradition. He disappeared for a few years. When we saw him again, we were no longer in Matiguás or were just about to leave. He was completely changed. No more shouting. He smiled and talked with us, shared our ideas, and tried to change all the old missionaries' habits. He became Provincial Superior of his order. Unfortunately, we were no longer at the mission

The Matiguas Mission—Successes and Failures

in Matiguás. I do not want be presumptuous—and I can't prove it—but that Father was saved by the discussions of the courageous missionary Sisters.

And I remembered Sister Juana Zoraida. One of the many times that I was in serious trouble because I didn't know who to send to Matiguás, I turned to Sister Juana Zoraida. We needed a director of the school when it was still in precarious condition. I called her, knowing that, although she was a wonderful missionary, she had a bad handicap. One leg was slightly shorter than the other. It wasn't a problem until she was about 35, when she was a folklore dancer and dance teacher. Now the leg gave her acute pain. Possibly she was about to need a prosthesis. Pushed by necessity, I tried to propose Matiguás to her. We talked for a long time until late at night. In the end we decided it just wasn't prudent. Matiguás would be the coup de grace for her poor leg.

The next morning, early, I was still in bed when she knocked on my bedroom door and told me that she had prayed a lot and decided to go to Matiguás. Was she a missionary for her own health? I was in tears when she left the next day.

Then I remembered Sister Felicia, already elderly, deaf, spending her days sewing in a room in our beautiful college in Diriambi. When we proposed the Matiguás mission, she didn't bat an eye. She got ready and left. She was the pioneer of the mission and a buffer between the Fathers and the Sisters, between the Sisters and the people, between the old

143

generation—she led a prayer group of older women—and the new, between the Contras and the Sandinistas. When she left, many things changed for the worse in Matiguás. Maybe she wasn't a vanguard Sister, but she was definitely a Sister of great religious spirit.

And Sister "Marcella." She had changed the system of health care and had taught responsibility, self-denial, and respect for all. Of course the fruits were yet to be seen, and perhaps we had a long time to wait.

The Matiguás mission went on a few more years. When I was transferred from Nicaragua to other places, the Sisters realized that they wouldn't be able to stay there much longer. They had been there for over ten years thanks to their own stubbornness, especially that of foreign Sisters. This was a phenomenon that we recognized every day. The Sisters were very respectable, but the conflicts destroyed them.

The mission was left to fend for itself. The Fathers didn't want to have anything to do with the school, so it went into the hands of the government. I do not know, and I never want to know, what happened to that beautiful clean, flowery school, with its orchard and vegetable garden. I believe that governmental neglect reduced it to a mess.

I never returned to Matiguás. There was no reason to go. I always avoided talking to the Sisters who considered the mission a painful interlude. The Fathers had called on other Sisters more in line with their way of thinking. They arrived

THE MATIGUAS MISSION—SUCCESSES AND FAILURES

while we were still there. Later I learned that the Fathers had re-opened the school, returning to their way of doing things and erasing the years of suffering that had meant to bring about some change. Maybe that was the right way to do it.

I still have indelible memories of long, tiring journeys, leaving from Managua at three in the morning to get to Matiguás at six or seven in the evening, dirty, dusty, battered by the jolts of the van, with aching bones and knees all bruised up from pushing them against the front seat to keep from falling over, and the long prayers made to sweet Saint Joseph when the microbus was broken down and I had to wait on the road for fate to give me a ride, maybe a truck carrying cows that made me travel holding my nose. The shower that I rushed to take when I arrived, with a bucket of rainwater while little frogs jumped all over, and pineapple or banana cake that dear Sister Felicia made me, and the unending suffering that I listened to without knowing of any solution.

After a few years I saw Sister Marcella again, now Mrs. Marcella. She asked me for forgiveness and a job. We hugged. I felt that she had found her identity and, after the storm, she realized where she belonged: in the missionary life.

I don't know whether the story of the Matiguás mission could be called a story of failure without considering the profoundly Christian thought that "some sow; others reap."

But it seems that the resonance that this experience has had on me is more complex. I have the impression that it symbolizes a reality that is often present in our lives, on its various planes and levels. A teacher can understand this a little. Among her pupils there is always someone who does not blossom, perhaps because it is perhaps not yet the right time. Often the teacher has the feeling that subjects administered in certain doses cannot penetrate the intellectual level of certain learners. Sometimes one understands, sometimes not, and that's why the student's frustration has no explanation.

Often I remain puzzled in the face of friendship. Maybe I always gave more than someone else could take in and therefore shied away because he or she expected less, much less. Or they backed off in the face of a more serious or radical solution that I myself wanted. They rejected me because the immediate and superficial solution was easier to accept. Or the view of events, carried to a higher and more universal plane, encounters a negative reaction in someone who is more comfortable looking only at the level of the particular or specific.

All the same, dozens of examples convince me that the experience of failure has a future that we can't see, while easy success, though good, does not help us move ahead. In the end, this discourse is banal, because many do help, but it has something mysterious that few can bear.

Second Intermission

In a passage of Deuteronomy it is written: "So be careful to do what the Lord your God has commanded you; do not turn aside to the right or to the left. Walk in obedience to all that the Lord your God has commanded you, so that you may live and prosper and prolong your days in the land that you will possess." (Dt 5: 32-33).

It was an insight that I had at the Bogotá airport.: Before us there are always two paths to choose from: those of the blessing and the curse, of good and evil (Dt. 30: 25-26), of life and death. I could not choose the path of self-pity or recrimination. Before me were God and his path. The rest made no difference except to make us realists.

The Central American experience had lasted just under ten years. I learned to size up my beliefs and my weaknesses. I vigorously dealt with difficult things, leaning on an ideal that became more concrete every day. The culture shock had *taught me to be objective, to look in the mirror and see in myself good things and less good things, true values and others that only seemed like values. One important value is that to live a vocation in a significant way, one must accept one's loneliness every day—not the sentimental kind that makes us feel the lack of friends and acquaintances, family members and peers, but that deep, unbridgeable loneliness that no one will ever reach across. This fact, highly personal, always represented my radical vulnerability together with the unattainable mystery of myself. When my heart broke free of the breathlessness of seeking fulfillment, I naturally opened myself to the needs of others, to the pain and emptiness that surrounds millions of people. My heart broke free thanks to the fact that I saw the importance of solitude as a value as well as a mystery.*

I remained like that, alone and with others, in an apparent contradiction, but the world and humanity came into my being, and transfigured me.

Many times I experienced the chasm that separates me from others, their ideas, their way of life, their customs and habits, shallowness and deceit. But then there were still others who made me discover my fundamental difficulty in understanding the wealth they had and the infinite burden of life with which they were endowed. So, little by little, I entered into a new synthesis in which God was revealed as the God of the poor.

On this issue I had had many experiences. I had to free myself from the tendency to maternalism and from believing

Second Intermission

myself capable of doing something useful. The younger Sisters taught me with their ability always to hope, that it was not enough to say, "poor thing, what can we do for him...." It was necessary to take on that poverty substantially, to make myself part of it, co-responsible, without prejudice, humbly accepting the lesson that it brought me.

The world of the poor was extremely difficult for me. The fact that those who most benefited would become the most rebellious, and that in a moment they would destroy things that had taken us years of sacrifice to build, and steal things and were always willing to deceive presented me with a fundamental choice: a pure, selfless, transcendent choice to be ready to give my life and not see the fruits of my efforts.

One day an Argentine Sister who had been in Nicaragua for eighteen years came to tell me, crying, that once again all the supplies of her crafts school, which had helped thousands of young people, had been stolen. The Sister wept with frustration, but she adored her mission. To console her I said that I found it difficult to understand people's ingratitude. She said simply that the option for the poor is not a social or emotional option, it's a theological option. I did not understand exactly what she meant, but I learned my lesson. To opt for the poor is to get into a mystery as mysterious as the God who became poor for us. He, God, demands nothing from us but with mercy bears every ingratitude.

My mission, therefore, created both an abyss and a closeness with the poor. I always had to choose my own inability to take on the option in full, and this, too, was loneliness.

I fought against my judgment, not by denying it—even at some point realizing that it was a gift—but by getting it to love before judging. I began to feel more deeply the mysterious communication with my founder, Madre Francesca Cabrini, who loved me without forcing me to change. Gradually, without realizing it, I became envious of everything that belonged to her. Even when I sensed hostility around me, I felt part of a family that was mine. Often, in situations negative toward me, a veil was spread before the eyes of my heart, and I could not see that well. It was a mess, in certain cases, but in many others it was my salvation.

I was now plunged into an extraordinary adventure. I saw before me a long and increasingly difficult road. Experience, however, had taught me to look, "neither right nor left," but straight in front of me, always following that distant point of light that kept me from getting lost in the tunnel. To expect neither approval nor esteem, neither praise nor encouragement, I just had to firmly believe in the One who fascinated me and not try to exploit it, but to get closer to Him, always removing my sandals, conscious that the mystery is not understood, and unreservedly trusting His word, the word that had been revealed and which pointed the way. This, then, was to be paid for with a long purification. It was unavoidable.

So it was that I learned to walk looking forward, dreaming

Second Intermission

and hoping even though those around me had not dreamed or hoped and preferred the status quo. The heavy burden of myself was losing significance. The Kingdom of God was giving me a more attractive and adventurous alternative. I had to immerse myself in it and let myself be dazzled by its beauty and its mystery.

I had been immersed in the reality of Central America. Now I emerged from that pool of light and realized that it would take some time to get into another reality and love it as much. But the future did not worry me. The reins of my fate had escaped from my hands. God had them, and when I loosened my grip, the torment of unnecessary complications began again. So I decided (so to speak) to let Him do it and let myself go ahead with other plans and other parameters, intrigued by this new adventure that was about to begin at the Bogotá airport.

11

A Sister Tired and Ill

In Argentina I was received coldly, even though I had good friends among the Sisters. Since they had been told that I was tired and sick, a Sister who came to get me at the airport said, "I thought you were on crutches." They sent me to rest in Cappilla del Monte, a delightful resort of the Sierra de Cordoba, in the center-north of Argentina. Even there, the young Superior, a dear Sister who had studied in Rome when I was there, too, said, "But if you are sick and need care, why did they send you here, a poor House without resources?" I did not reply because it wasn't worth it. I struggled to adapt even though the climate was supposed to be good, because it was very cold. When we arrived, it was eight degrees below zero celsius and the House was poorly heated while I had become accustomed to the heat I'd felt for ten years in Central America.

In the modest reception I received, Mother Clemens made an exception. She was a nice French Sister of 84 years. Her kindness and warmth compensated by far the coldness of the others. Serene and spiritual, she invited me to sit next to her in front of a big stove which they called "the salamander." While chatting, she was trying to understand what illness I was suffering and why I had been sent there.

In Argentina I was present for the end of its military government, which was on its last legs. I had come at the most crucial time, when the wound still burned from the useless war for the Falkland Islands and the military was bankrupt and on its way out.

When the Provincial Superior came—whom I still hadn't seen though I knew her very well—she told me that I could take care of pastoral vocations, the formation of some young aspirants to religious life, and anything else that came up. This sounded a bit strange, but I replied that I would do my best.

I found some very dear people with whom I formed a good relationship, but the situation of the Province was very fluid and elusive. I began to travel a lot, always by bus, traveling long distances across the flat, plain pampas of Argentina, moving from one Community to another as I began the vocational activity that I had to improvise as I went along. Nobody wanted to finance this work, and I always had to deal with money, which

A Sister Tired and Ill

ran out when I was a long way away. This was because of the terrible inflation. If one day 100 pesos was enough for a trip, the next day I needed 200. I discovered the wealth of the secular world close to our mission, though I had to be very careful not to use my language of liberation. It had been forbidden in Argentina and was still not in use among the people. The fact that I had come from Nicaragua—which, according to them, was a communist country—clashed with a mentality that had been punished by years of military rule.

I was able to devote myself to reading (a Sister who had been my novice gave me books) and to prayer, discovering again the beauty of the Bible that revealed to me the path of Moses for the liberation of his people. Strangely enough, I applied this information to the situation of our Institute. I read everything that was coming out about the military government: the concentration camps, torture, "disappearances," the terrible corruption, denouncing, and deception. But the Sisters found it hard to believe and admit those things. I think my boldness in making known the things that I read and the fact that I opened myself to them too soon helped to make me less likable. The lay people were more open and welcoming, and with the very young I was especially able to initiate some activities. Soon, however, I had to realize that the same people who welcomed my initiative remained silent with the other Sisters because I represented a transitional figure. They were aware that everything would depend on others.

To the Ends of the Earth

My readings, which were many, for the most part concerned religious life. They were books published by CLAR, which was a spearhead of religious life in Latin America, books that were just beginning to enter Argentina because they had been banned. I read studies, analyses, and research, and I realized that religious life was at a turning point. Not only that, but the books were outlining two or three major strands: the purely traditional, the progressive, and a trend that was in the middle. All three were looking for a new definition that would take years to reach. Accustomed as I was to comparison, analysis, and open discussion, I suffered a lot to have discussions only with Sisters and lay people who were more critical of the situation. Also for this I was regarded with suspicion, and, to ingratiate.

Spring arrived. The scenic beauty of the sierra made me forget all the suffering, every bit of homesickness for my memories of Nicaragua. Beauty has always played a fundamental part inside me. A beautiful sunset or a starry night in which I could see—what satisfaction!—the Southern Cross, or seeing peach trees blooming a beautiful pink, or the gurgle of a nearby stream that seemed like a song, or the beautiful fabrics of local crafts, or music like the true Argentine tango, I enjoyed enormously. From Nicaragua and Guatemala I heard only sporadic news. Mother Clemens, who was the first to read the newspaper, marked with a dot the articles that she now knew would interest me most. I spent the morning praying and reading the paper. Then I took long walks in the neighborhood,

A Sister Tired and Ill

starting a kind of little mission among the poorest people.

Early summer in Argentina coincided with Christmas. I was invited to Buenos Aires by Mother Antoinetta, my former Regional Superior, who was in Central America before the revolution. Mother Antoinetta was very affectionate. Years before she had taken me to see Mendoza, a beautiful city in the north. I remained in her Community until after Christmas. In preparation for Christmas I started up a novena celebrated by families. This enthused Mother Antoinetta. She had us go from house to house for nine days to people's great satisfaction.

The New Year brought a great event for the Institute. The General Chapter—a meeting of leading missionary Sisters of the Sacred Heart from all over the world—would be celebrated. A new Superior General was to be elected. I was invited by the Provincial Superior to take part in the preparation of the Provincial Chapter there in Argentina. I found myself working with Sisters who had no great enthusiasm; they said it was always the same things, which were never seen carried out. There were speeches so depressing that the Sisters felt like running away. But my reading had prepared me. What I saw was a situation that I had found in many studies I had analyzed: a lot of Sisters immersed in institutional work no longer found time to express the prophecy. When this coincided at a critical time, a loss of meaning occurred. I was alarmed. At the same time, something inside made me see the positive in everything that others saw as negative. Although I was neither part of nor a member of the Provincial Chapter, I think I contributed to the preparation with some effect.

A few months later, the Provincial Superior informed me that the Mother General wanted me to participate as an invited Sister in the General Chapter that would be celebrated in July. It seemed absurd. Why? I had been dismissed from my post in Nicaragua for serious reasons, and now I was invited to the General Chapter, which is reserved for the most accepted people! I replied that it did not seem appropriate, that I was grateful but had made other commitments, and I had to deal with them. There was in me a kind of bewilderment. I understood that this invitation was a kind of "making up," but there was nothing I could do. The Mother General insisted. I had to go.

In Rome I found the atmosphere rather strange. They looked at me in a certain way. I could not understand what was behind it. My usual naiveté prevented me from asking questions. I thought that maybe everyone saw on my forehead the red and black flag of the Sandinistas!

Since I was only a non-voting invitee, I knew that during the election of the Superior General I had to stay out. So I got a ticket to go to Sicily to visit my Sister, who was on holiday. But the Superior General didn't allow me to leave. I felt the atmosphere tense and polemic. According to some Sisters, this was due, in part, because in the Institute, psychology had become the standard by which to measure the vocations, values, and ability of people, their maturity in the faith, and issues like that. In

A Sister Tired and Ill

fact that was a bit of an exaggeration of certain psychological techniques, but I wasn't worried. I liked psychology. It helped me a lot in my job training. Some Sisters asked my opinion, and I explained that this was not a problem that should be treated at a Chapter. The Institute had far more serious problems that were putting its survival at stake.

The election phase began. I stayed in the back, praying a little, doing a crossword a little. Then I began to hear my name among the candidates. Concern and tranquility alternated in me. I didn't have much time to analyze my feelings. I remember that I asked myself: "What reasons do you have to withdraw? Do it while you still have time!" I had so many answers, but all were vague. There are times when you feel reluctant to respond. Then I asked myself, "What reasons compel you to accept?" The answer that came to me was: the poor and Latin America. But I did not know what I was saying. A few minutes later I heard the outgoing Superior General say: "Sisters—Sister Maria Barbagallo is our Superior General." Then a thunderous applause broke out. I was beginning another adventure.

12

The New Ways of the Religious Life

I had to take the reins of the Chapter, and I did it with great ease, to the point that a Sister said, "Tell the truth, you expected to be elected." Yes, perhaps she was right, I expected it.

There had been inside me, in the previous months, a strange serenity, an inexplicable urge to read and prepare, an unusual desire to learn about new missionary cases and new ways of religious life. But it certainly wasn't all that explicit.

The Chapter continued with new plans based mainly on the mission and the option for the poor.

At first I thought to devote myself to the missionary life, getting back to the fundamentals in new territory to push the prophecy and the gospel, all with a touch of idealism. But after my first visit to all (or almost all) the Institute Communities, I had a disturbing sensation.

A Shakespeare play came to mind. In it, a king, on the eve of a major battle, wanted to make a turn through his soldiers' encampment. In the evening, disguised, he began to go among the soldiers. They were discouraged and dejected. Some were thinking of deserting, others looked for women, others got drunk. The king realized that the battle of the next day would be a defeat. He decided to devote himself to his soldiers. Although my situation wasn't as serious, I realized that most of the Sisters were resigned to the inevitable end toward which the Institute was falling. This perception was compounded by the inexorable aging of the members and the lack of vocations. Almost all the missions had serious difficulty to survive, and many were in the process of closing.

The psychological state of the Congregation had taken away the self-confidence of many Sisters. They no longer believed themselves capable of anything. Everybodyelse seemed was more qualified than them, and at their age, there was no longer anything to expect. Many Houses were in decline. The theory that what matters is the mission had obscured the exterior aspect, and there was a sense of abandonment in many communities. I was frightened to hear many elderly Sisters say, "We're too old. We no longer have value. Our Institute is coming to an end!"

I devoted myself to the Sisters. I found in them great spiritual

The New Ways of the Religious Life

values but a bit faded, and I realized that it was necessary to restore confidence and bring back the Cabrini motto: "I can do everything through Him who strengthens me." It was necessary to reorganize the work and the Community, to trust lay people, to discover new vocations and lay workers, and liberate oneself from the death complex that seemed to have infected us.

We organized training sessions on the Cabrini spirit and the missionary sense of life. I especially devoted myself to the more adult Sisters. The few young people were too pampered! It was hard work. I realized that we had to change our language, our way of thinking, the criteria of evangelization, and our style of Community. It was necessary to give a new meaning to people, Communities and projects. It was not easy.

I worked all the time, without rest, without holidays, without Saturdays and Sundays. I tried to revive the great figure of Mother Cabrini in Sisters and lay people. Many Sisters confessed that they had never read the whole biography of Mother Cabrini! I tried to use imagination in meetings, in liturgy and language in order to show examples of our missionary life. But it took a lot of grit. Change, which everyone wanted in theory, was not so welcome in practice. I had to use viclence and provocation. Many firm plans remained only that. The Sisters did not understand that every passing day could be fatal. And in many cases it was.

My meetings with the Sisters and the missions created no end of problems, but also a lot of satisfaction that is hard to describe. It was fed by missionary activities that I saw carried out. It wasn't true that we were going to die! There was great vitality everywhere. Every so often I was attacked by fear of not taking advantage of it.

Travel, especially by plane.—I've always been afraid of airplanes!—tired me terribly. I traveled constantly, and when I returned to Rome, it was to prepare for the next trip and the work to be done at the next destination.

I became familiar with airports, stations and trains, buses, and places. The continuous travelling forced me into a certain asceticism: the fatigue, the different time zones, the lack of time to rest and digest the experience that I had just finished before immediately throwing myself into another, the diversity of culture and mentality, the different customs (we dine at 5..., we dine at 9...!), the changes in food and climate, of always having to give up my preferences, my habits, my wishes, and my ideas. Others, the ones who received me, did not always understand my physical and mental discomfort after a flight of 10 or 15 hours or a bus or train trip of hours and hours, or of being tossed around in a terrible jeep on terrible roads and then hearing "We do it all the time!" Different houses, different beds, different people, different places. I had to maintain a logical thread in myself so as to not lose my orientation.

The trips involved ventures that were sometimes dangerous, sometimes interesting or funny. Sometimes, just as I arrived at an airport or train station, the people who were picking me up

The New Ways of the Religious Life

launched into a litany of problems. Other times, thinking they were doing me a favor, they organized a dinner with so and so, or a surprise.

Once I arrived in Denver at nine p.m., or later. Because of a blizzard, I had to wait a few hours for someone to come pick me up. More than a meter of snow had fallen. I had come from Italy, with a layover of three or four hours in Miami. When finally the Sisters came to collect us (I was with Madre Lina, a dear friend and companion of adventures), it was after eleven. They told me that we could not go straight home because a Sister was dying in the hospital and she wanted to see me at all costs. We went to the hospital. The Sister was surrounded by friends and acquaintances. When she saw me she began a great speech of thanks to the Lord for the grace of seeing me before she died. Mother Lina, said to me softly, "This Sister is in better health than us. . . let's get out of here." She lived several more years.

Another time, arriving in Philadelphia late at night, I thanked God I didn't have to see anybody. I took a shower and slipped into bed, dead tired. I was about to fall asleep when someone knocked. A Sister came in with great, American-style exclamations, "Welcome, oh, but you're here! We didn't know, come on, let's go!" She got me out of bed to show me some pictures of a Sister and little things of that kind.

When I traveled to Central America, something always happened. I got stuck in Madrid, or Miami, or Panama. Alone at an airport for hours, sometimes I was even afraid. Once I arrived in Panama at four in the morning and I had no connecting flight until six in the evening. By chance, the Bishop of Panama passed by. He was going to Rome. He asked me what I was waiting for. When he heard how long I had to stay there, he had me taken to a diocese house to rest. A very pretty young lady picked me up and offered me breakfast, then told me she had to leave. She took me with her. After accompanying her to various chores, she had me wait on the road more than two hours and then, finally, took me back to the airport!

On a trip from Swaziland to Johannesburg, we took a small plane which flew at low altitude to try to avoid a storm. Unfortunately, a few minutes before landing, we were caught in the middle of the storm and we were tossed by the wind for over an hour inside that little iron cylinder.

But there were plenty of encounters with people who were immediately friendly despite my tendency to avoid relationships. I learned many lessons from common people. The journeys by land were even more complicated and exhausting. Once, at the Honduran border, I was waiting for the endless inspection of suitcases. I was approached by an elderly and very subdued woman. Accustomed to seeing people begging, I tried several times to discourage the woman. But the poor woman kept following me and seeing my indifference (may God forgive me!), she said, "Sister, when one wants to talk, it's not always to ask for money. Sometimes one needs a word of comfort." Humiliated and confused by that terrible lesson, I sat on a low wall to talk to her. The poor woman told me about her terrible situation: three men had entered her home and killed her husband in his sleep. One of her children, the youngest, had not been seen by the criminals and had recognized the men. The eldest children had forced him to speak, and now they were preparing revenge. The poor woman explained to me that it was one more crime of revenge. She wanted to put an end to the tragic chain once and for all. "Someone," she said, "has to start to forgive." She wanted me to pray for her.

The trips taught me to listen, which is real, which is friendship. On a trip from Nicaragua to Guatemala, as usual by land, a man tried several times to speak with me, but I discouraged him because I wanted to rest and read. As I read, I sensed my rudeness and selfishness, so I buttonholed him. The man was very intelligent and had read many books of foreign literature. He told me his whole life. He had been abandoned by his parents when he was very small, and he never saw them again. He wandered around the Nicaraguan port of Corinto, sneaking and scraping around for something to eat. At night he slept in any old corner. A man, a customs officer who lived alone, picked him up and became his Father. He taught the boy to read, to write, to wash, to work, but above all to be a man. Reading a long time, watching the sea in sunny and stormy days, traveling and dealing with men of every kind, he developed a philosophy. "Life," he told me, "is my philosophy, my religion and my reason for living, because the man who taught me taught me that being a thief, a scoundrel, a beggar is to give up living. To live, you have to be a man." Then he wanted to know about my life, my vows, my religion. He had never heard of Jesus in a concrete way. When we parted he said, "You know, at first, you looked like a very disagreeable person... but now, I have changed my mind."

I cannot help but recall a curious thing that happened to me during a stopover at the airport in Rio de Janeiro. I was coming from Italy and waiting for my flight to Sao Paulo. As usual I was numb from the ten-hour flight, from sleepiness and the frustration of not finding a real cup of coffee in the country of coffee. A man approached with his wife, a typical couple from the southern United States—he in plaid pants and white shoes, she in purple suit with a bowl of curls on her head. They greeted me very politely and began to talk about their situation. They were also on a layover but were arriving from the United States. They had come to Brazil to look for an institution that would treat children suffering from multiple sclerosis. Their only son had died of that disease. They had spent their lives going from one hospital to another, one specialist to another. Now they were alone and had decided to donate their fortune to a needy hospital or institution. The man insisted on asking if we had a similar hospital. I explained that we had hospitals and organizations for children but not precisely for that disease. I tried to make myself understood with my poor English, but the man, despite his wife trying to explain what I was saying, opened his briefcase and took out a donation document, everything in order, with signatures and stamps. He wanted me to read it. I was shocked because my eyes went immediately to the sum: three million dollars! I was not wrong. As I tried to explain and to promise that I would look into it and was going to give them instructions, the man continued to tell me that they were giving the money to me, to my Congregation. And I was saying no, we had no such organizations for children with multiple sclerosis. He got out of that terrible commitment when the loudspeaker called for passengers, both for me and for my unusual donors. During the trip I thought of a title for a *Reader's Digest* article: Rejecting three million dollars!

The unforeseeable on trips, which should have been out of the ordinary, became the ordinary to the point that now I was prepared for anything—to be told at the ticket counter, "But you are not booked," even though I had made the reservation a year earlier. Or, "But you can't travel with this ticket; you have to pay another 600 dollars." Or, "But you don't have a visa." Or "But you will have to stay the night here, there's no flight until tomorrow." I learned to be tough, never to accept a demand for more payments, never to give in to the first "No," to continuously stand up for my rights. But a lot of times I had to let it go. Suitcases always weighing more than the famous 20 kilos were another problem to struggle with on every trip.

There were all kinds of problems when I had to take a taxi in the evening or at night, or to look for a hotel at night.

To the Ends of the Earth

Running into drunks and people with bad intentions, I always prayed to St. Joseph to get me out of the situation. Crossword puzzles, solitaire, chess and checkers when I had a friend, knitting needles, books to read, were all part of traveling and using time well. But it was through true asceticism that I found meaning in these trips.

But when I arrived at a mission, I forgot everything. I was pulled into the plight of the poor, in the heroic difficulties of so many Sister missionaries, in the impotence that we all experienced when, after struggling so much, the rewards were meager. In addition to the missionary aspect, what gave me wings was the deepening of the charism of Mother Cabrini, the opening to the laity, the Gospel reflection of the reality that we were experiencing. On these issues, I have abided, with satisfaction, days and nights, travel and energy.

Each missionary area had its special characteristics. In Brazil I was always overcome by the missions inserted among the poor. The Sisters always led me to recognize reality, the harder and more dramatic one.

I learned a lot from the Brazilian Sisters—their sensitivity to social problems, the marginalized, the poor, the "impoverished," as they used to say. Their songs of liberation, their liturgies (sometimes very long) with large Congregations, their analysis of reality and their theological reflection on everyday life—even though I'd been through all that in my Central American experience. I remembered that on my first trip to Brazil, Mother Lucia led me to know the most beautiful things. On that occasion I visited a ranch that was a charm. It looked like a huge garden in which grew all kinds of plants, flowers and fruits. It was crossed by a river where ships passed loaded with goods to be exported. There were even families of former slaves who lived in beautiful modern houses. Much time had passed. Our missionary awareness had changed. The Sisters were no longer interested in ranches or, if they were, it was to criticize their system of injustice. The Sisters were now following the story of the people. I remember a Sister who was committed to the pastoral care of the earth, often accompanying landless people to gain their rights through peaceful means, with prayers, with protest movements that were sometimes very dangerous, because these were not activities liked by big landowners who deployed their own security forces.

What I really loved were the ecclesiastical base communities. It was truly a pleasure to see humble people pray, reflect and discuss the problems they suffered. I admired their ability to denounce injustice and deal with conflicts to defend human rights.

In the United States, I became fond of many projects in which I still felt the presence of Mother Cabrini, especially the organizations for immigrants. Besides their internal work, hospitals held outside activities in the most marginalized areas of the city with clinics for various groups of people: Mexicans, Chinese, blacks. The world of migrants came into my life as the world of the poor had done when I was in Latin America. Once I went to pray in the room where Mother Cabrini had died, in her sanctuary in Chicago. There was a large glass bowl in which people left little notes with requests for grace they hoped for from Mother Cabrini. I was alone and the sanctuary was closed to the public. I started reading some hundreds of those tickets, which aroused pain mixed with tenderness. Most said: "Mother Cabrini, please, let me get a job... let me learn the language because no one will give me work... let me get a place to live... don't let them find out where I live... my son takes drugs, mother help him find the right path... my husband has cancer..." I did nothing but stay to pray for these people, as oppressed now as they were at the time of Cabrini.

In New York, I was deeply struck by a department of our hospital called Cabrini Hospice. It was for the terminally ill. It was founded by a priest, who then died there. It aims to assist people at the point when the disease can no longer be treated by the family, or when the patient is in and out of the hospital. Most are young people aged twenty to thirty years with AIDS or cancer. The Sister who collaborates in their care, especially spiritual, had profound experience with death and the way many people approach it. Often these young people, usually abandoned by their families, die in her arms because she wants them to feel "the embrace of the Father who receives them." This Sister was often invited to speak to medical school students. Once a student raised his hand to say, "Sister, if I

The New Ways of the Religious Life

must die, I want to die in your arms." At West Park, I was struck by the mission to the abandoned young men and women, the affectionate and intelligent way they were rehabilitated, the vitality of the mission. At Radnor, the magnificent university, and then Denver, New Orleans, Seattle—many Cabrini places and memories, Sisters and lay people struck me with their sense of belonging to a history that was still going strong.

Africa made me relive my youthful dreams. I was fortunate to visit a venerable old man, the first Christian catechist in Swaziland. Every place I visited conquered me entirely.

In Italy I was especially in love with Codogno, the first House of the Institute. Every time I came back from a long trip, I liked to go to Codogno, to relive that Cabrinian spirit that always impassioned me. Italian Sisters, the older ones, were a delight when they told me about their missionary adventures.

Spain, England, France and the new missions in Switzerland and Portugal—everything had a special attraction for me.

My two trips to Australia made me even more aware of the capabilities of the laity to take the Cabrini spirit and put it into practice. Even though we had few Sisters there, I had the consolation of seeing projects carried out by lay people who had lived with the Sisters for many years.

Certainly it wasn't just the missionary activities but the many problems related to them that required my serenity and understanding. The Sisters there generally had to live amid the great difficulties of every day. In the evening, when I came home and I could finally be alone in my room, I felt a burst of emotion. Sometimes I cried for joy, sorrow, hope, or the disturbance that I felt with the news of a beautiful mission closing because for infinite reasons it could not go on.

The first six-year term was rich with events, conflicts, suffering and frustration. My closest collaborators helped me a lot, but sometimes they understood me, sometimes not. I had to get used to the stress of seeing resistance to even simple things—simple to me, anyway. Also because the missions and provinces had autonomy and direct influence over local situations, things were always difficult. I had to wait for the tempo of others, to bear criticism—justified or unjustified—to accept seeing an opportunity lost because the others were not willing to go along.

Along came the next General Chapter, where I might or might not be re-elected. I prepared very carefully, but for some things the time was not yet ripe. The new thing was the participation of the laity and with it the concrete proposal to have lay missionaries in the Cabrini Congregation. There were three of them present. I called them one by one and asked them, "Do you feel you can fulfill your formal promise as a lay missionary in the Chapter?" All three said *Yes*. They were two married ladies and a girl who later became a Sister. It was a beautiful thing. It made up for my many disappointments. I was re-elected.

13

Loneliness and Hope

I approached the second six-year term as Superior General with more awareness. When I was elected the first time I enjoyed a certain ignorance of things and this gave me an excess of optimism and therefore an excess of frustrations. Now I knew a lot more. I knew the Sisters, the missions, the difficulties and the risks. Now I knew that I couldn't make miracles. But I went ahead with enthusiasm. I was sustained by God and by the prayers of many Sisters, especially the older ones. They were my consolation, and each time one died, I was left with a terrible emptiness. I was also sustained by the goals that I wanted to achieve, by the emergence of lay vocations, and by the many volunteers who wished to collaborate, however sporadically.

Above all, I experienced great hope. I don't know where it came from, when everybody talked about nothing but problems, difficulties, and things that could not be accomplished. There was something like a light inside me that showed me little solutions, roads, and initiatives, a light that let me see the positive, as had happened to me in the past. Sometimes I happened to be at a dead end and didn't know what to do while other people expected an immediate answer. And then I experienced, almost unexpectedly, an inner light that helped me, and along came a solution—perhaps precarious, perhaps temporary, but it came and it worked. My ordeal was always the loneliness. Others often did not see it the same way. But things went on. New missions opened, made their way forward with hard work. Through a process of re-founding, we approached a new missionary vision long cultivated in my dreams and the dreams of many others.

Another experience that stayed with me was the knowledge that I was on the right path and the courage not to give up even if I saw people around me unconvinced, and some hints of defeatism. By that time I learned that other people are willing to accompany me when they foresee success. I, on the other hand, had to act even when success was absolutely uncertain. I consoled myself by saying: "Maria, this thing will probably go wrong, but you must be ready to say, 'I was wrong.'" I made myself an ongoing catechesis!

Loneliness and Hope

On the other hand, I had to have a little consideration for myself. I had no time to digest events. I had to withdraw to pray, to reflect, sometimes to distract myself. I had to avoid working at night and wasting energy on things that were not necessary, such as invitations, dinners, or walks. Relationships with other people were hard on me. Sometimes I couldn't establish the right contact. These relationships required time, effort and my help. I always saw myself as doing my best while others complained that I didn't give them enough time. Once I traveled almost twenty hours with a Sister. During the trip we talked at length, and I listened for many hours. A few days later she told me that I never found time for her. This seemed strange, but it was a situation that was repeated. People don't want random time; they want dedicated time.

One experience that has made me reflect a lot is the diversity of understanding brought about by different degrees of maturity. Often I felt that using the same language does not mean understanding if we are at different levels. For example, believing in cooperation does not mean that we know how to cooperate correctly. Maybe it would be better if someone works alone. I often found myself in this situation. I had to do a whole group's work, spending a lot of energy. I had to do everything. Sometimes, to make something acceptable, I had to lie and say someone else had done it. I did film, theater, articles, translations, homilies, reflections, letters. I was quite surprised to hold up through so much work while others succumbed to

To the Ends of the Earth

fatigue.

But, between limits, failures, satisfaction and all sorts of results, it was six years of a nomadic life replete with responsibility, light, and darkness.

Along came the 1996 Chapter. My term ended. I had to prepare everything and prepare myself for another dive into the void. The Chapter began with the usual concern over electing a new General Superior. This, too, required a lot of work, before and during and after the vote. Mother Lina Colombini, a good person, was elected, though almost no one expected it. I hope to have the time, before dying, to tell how she was elected, but it's still early for that. Mother Lina was my faithful collaborator for 12 years. I loved her very much, even if our opinions sometimes differed. I affectionately called her "Linoleum." When she was elected, she wept so much that I thought she would burst. She was not prepared though there were prophets who had spoken her name all over the world. A few days after her election, I said, "Mother …", she paused and tearfully said, "Call me Linoleum …."

When the Chapter ended, I had the strange sensation of being suspended in time. I had no past, which was over in a flash, and no future, as no one thought about what would come next for me. I took care of a few important things so I could completely leave that job behind. My only certainty was that I had to move to a new home. Many people asked me: where will you go now?

Loneliness and Hope

But I did not know exactly. I had that luminous porthole in front of me. The rest, as always, was darkness. Meanwhile, I would be gone to Romania for a few months to distance myself and to look into other possibilities.

14

A Parenthetical Pause

In early September 1996, I left for Romania in the company of a Sister who had agreed to share this pseudo-holiday with me. I was taking the vacation to separate myself a little from the environment in which I had lived intense apostolic and missionary activity for twelve years.

I chose Romania for two reasons: first, I was responding to an urgent call that had been made by a Romanian Congregation of Sisters who had been our guests in Rome for many years. After the fall of Ceausescu in 1989, the Romanian Church had asked various Congregations that were housed in Rome to host the Romanian Sisters who wanted to renew the theological and cultural preparations they had had to give up during the communist dictatorship and the subsequent religious persecution. We missionaries made our congregation available, and we welcomed in our religious Roman communities about ten Romanian Sisters belonging to a religious congregation that had been founded in prison at the time of the communist dictatorship.

The other reason was the desire to test the missionary fields that had opened in that region, already entered by other Congregations, with the eventual prospect of opening a mission in Romania. This possibility had led me to take a trip to Romania a few years before, almost immediately after the fall of the dictator. We made the trip by car, a Fiat 600 that broke down several times. We had a Sister to guide us. With her and another Sister, we ventured out from Rome, through Austria and Hungary, to reach Romania. We made it to Bucharest and were accepted by our friends, the Sisters. We spent a week discovering a city that had just emerged from communism with a vague regained freedom—no one wanted to talk about the recent past— with almost empty shops, restaurants where you could eat only pickles and little else. After that first trip, we proposed to return with more time and determination. On that occasion, the Sisters who had hosted us, who were very good and very poor, gave us their best room to sleep in, with three beds close to each other. It was next to their chapel, where people prayed night and day.

We left for Bucharest early in the month of September.

Parenthetical Pause

Sister Amelia—the Sister who had agreed to come with me—and I knew that we were not going to accomplish great things, but for me it would be a time of rest—especially mental rest—and a novelty for her, since she had never left Italy and was convinced that we were leaving on a mission. I brought with me a new computer that had been given to me and which I had just learned to use. The writer and friend Lucetta Scaraffia had given me the task of writing a few pages about my experience of life as a religious missionary.

Our good Romanian Sisters were waiting at the airport. They took us to their house and offered us a fairly large room where their aspiring young religious slept. One side of the room remained separate, as if it were a small adjoining room. The room was near a new bathroom. There was no shower but it had some precarious possibilities for washing oneself. Once again the Sisters made available the best they had, but we had planned to rent an apartment. At first, however, we tried to adapt without major problems. After the usual pleasantries and a few days of rest, the Sisters who hosted us helped us to know the city, to take public transportation, to go into the Catholic Church of the Latin rite that was the cathedral of Bucharest, as many Catholic churches were Eastern Rite. They also offered to teach us the Romanian language. We ate with them food we weren't used to, very fatty and poor. It often consisted of a large pot of soup with vegetables, meat and beans. They put the pot in the middle of the dining table, then went to pray for half an hour. Then they

183

sat at the table. When we didn't go out, we retreated to our little corner in the room to pray, read, or to make comments. This was on the first few days. In general, however, we went out to go to Mass and then to know the city.

The city of Bucharest had improved significantly compared to when I first visited. The transportation service was good, the stores better stocked, the restaurants more inviting, but there weren't many to choose from. What I found positive was the fact that in Romania there was a bread culture. Fresh bread was sold throughout the day, even on Saturdays and Sundays. In front of bakeries, always open, there were lines of people waiting for the bread to come out of the oven. We met many people with a long baguette in hand, as seen in France. This, for Sister Amelia and me, constituted an important resource. Eating little at meals, with the fresh bread we bought, which was very good, we reached a good balance of calories that we otherwise could not have provided to our bodies.

Our desire, however, was to have a bit of autonomy because we did not want to disturb the Sisters, who were very busy. Almost all, in fact, were busy working outside the Congregation to earn a living. We ourselves wanted to do our investigation freely.

The Sisters who hosted us were very kind, good, and willing to help us in every way. They especially hoped that our stay in Romania would end up opening a mission, and they helped us consider various possibilities, taking us to hospitals, homes for orphaned children, and priests they knew.

The young Sister—I'll call her Sister Magdalen— was just over eighteen and still a novice. She was endowed with special mystical gifts and wielded a powerful influence on people thanks to her deep spirituality and missionary ability. In prison she comforted priests and nuns, young people and adults, and she exhorted everyone to faithfulness and patience for that sad period the Church of Romania was enduring.

These Sisters belong to a religious Congregation, as I mentioned, founded in jail by a young woman religious belonging to another Congregation. She had been arrested, as had hundreds of others, because she was Catholic.

Sometimes she was released for short periods, but then she was arrested again because the regime feared her proselytizing. In prison, since she could have no contact with her Congregation, she thought of associating everyone who wanted to experience a new style of religious life. Young people and adults, men or women, priests, married or unmarried, could be part of the Congregation. The religious make-up was diversified. One could choose contemplation with perpetual adoration of the Blessed Sacrament, or the apostolic life living in the Community or at home. Members could be married, and so on. Because of her extraordinary ability to attract and call people together, the prison regime kept her under control, isolating her and often making her suffer physical, psychological, and moral torture, even threatening to kill her. But the girl did not give in.

The Sisters say that the priests who were in prison, when not closely watched, were able to celebrate the Eucharist. Everyone participated, and they also witnessed miraculous phenomena by virtue of this young religious woman.

Once during her sad isolation in a dark and putrid room, where, the Sisters told us, the young woman received visits of Our Lady, a jailer guard moved by her serenity and perseverance, asked how she could help. The young Sister told her that she would be very grateful to take Holy Communion, and whenever possible she would like a consecrated Host. The young woman also gave indications of where the guard could find the holy wafer. For a long time this satisfied the Sister. The guard brought the Host, which was procured at a clandestine church, hidden inside the bun of her hair.

Later, when her supervisors became suspicious, the woman had to interrupt her mission and, under precise instructions from Sister Maddalena, she decided to move out of Romania. When Maddalena arrived in Bucharest, the lady was still out of the country in fear of reprisals by the former regime, which still had some involvement in the government.

After the persecution, when Sister Maddalena was released from prison, a large group of followers gathered. She dedicated herself to organizing the various areas of her new Congregation, attracting many other young people. They were fascinated by her traumatic experience, but beyond that they were also rich in faith and Christian hope. Free from constraints, Sister Maddalena proved her great organizational skills and management and the spirit of ecclesiastical faith as she sought the approval of the Church. Unfortunately, at the time she wasn't given much credibility. Often the same priests who had followed her in prison, one of whom had become a bishop, would no longer support her in fear of being accused of being visionaries. This caused her pain, but at the same time brought her closer to the Passion of Jesus. The situation brought the Sister many consolations. When we met, she wore a turban that covered part of her forehead, and her hands were bound up, a sign of the wounds that the Crucified Lord had received. Another sign of her particular participation in the Passion of Jesus was her prolonged fast—we were told that she was not taking food and drink of any kind. Her adoration of the Holy Sacraments was on the day and night of every Thursday. It was she who, at first, in obedience to the Church, had sent her Sisters to Rome and other Italian cities to study. She was very grateful to us for accepting them.

We spent that first period of our stay in Romania learning in more detail the miraculous formation of the new congregation. The Sisters spoke little of those extraordinary events that they had lived through in prison or in hiding. But from various pamphlets and certain confidences the Sisters shared, we learned some very sad things. But we also learned some very beautiful things.

People talked little of the years of the dictatorship. Indeed, they did not talk about it at all. If you mentioned the issue, the subject was immediately changed. The time of the regime was still too recent. What they called the Securitate, or secret police, included people who were still living among them, and still had a lot of power, so we tried to learn things from foreign people, with whom we had some contacts.

One thing impressed me. Wwhile I criticized the ugliness of thousands of residential buildings. They all looked the same, like huge beehives of concrete. These buildings had taken the place of small, modest houses and cottages, though some of thes eoriginal houses were still visible in the peripheral areas of the city. Tthe Sisters who lived there appreciated the new buildings because, they said, at least they allowed everyone to have a home. Similarly, they much appreciated the huge building Ceausescu had built on the great Plaza of the Revolution, one of the largest in the world. They told us many things about it that were certainly not pleasant. The only thing you could really appreciate was the large fountain, which gave a little lightness to the group of huge buildings. Monasteries and churches that survived the regime, along with some houses and old buildings, made some areas of the city beautiful.

Of course, Sister Amelia and I continued to look for a small apartment that would allow us to live independently, but the Sisters who hosted us didn't want us to spend money. Rents were very expensive, so much so that it was almost worth buying an apartment. They insisted on this option, convincing that it would serve as a first step in our mission to Romania. Meanwhile, Mother Magdalene, hearing of our intention to rent an apartment, offered us a house that had been entrusted to her by the owner, who was the prison guard who had helped her during her imprisonment and was now in the United States.

So it was that, a few weeks after we arrived—it was at the end of September—we moved into this house, which was quite nice. It was located on a road not too central to the city, next to similar homes, with a small front yard. In one corner of the yard there was a rustic woodshed, storeroom and dog kennel. The entrance was through a kitchen off a small porch. The house had a large room, but it was locked with all the furniture inside. The small kitchen also served as a dining-room. There was a bathroom and another room with two beds in opposite corners, while in another corner there was a closet, and in the fourth corner there was a big stove of refractory bricks. This was our bedroom for about two and a half months. The stove was our salvation from the cold, which came quickly. We had to carefully keep it going, clean it, get wood from the yard, etc. Of course, all this fell to me because Sister Amelia was not really suitable for household chores. Likewise with the shopping, cooking, cleaning and so on. Among other things, we also had to look after the dog that guarded the house. Our friends, the Sisters, never let us lack a necessity. They brought us pepper sauce they'd made, and it was very good. The also brought cucumbers and cabbage that was cooked and very well prepared. Cabbage was a food that they cooked often. They preserved it for winter in big holes in the ground. We had excellent soups and very simple things. They liked nothing more than sweets, so I prepared an excellent tiramisu with delicious biscuits that were at the market, or fruit salad or ice cream. A couple of times we invited all the Romanian Sisters to dinner, but we went to their house to cook because we didn't have the necessary utensils. All 12 of them ate, and they were quite pleased with our Italian dishes.

When we were at home, I tried to use the computer to write about the experiences of my missionary life while Sister Amelia read all the pamphlets in Italian that the Sisters gave her. We prayed together and we commented on the Word of God. But she wanted to go out, talk and get to know new things, while I tended to stay quiet at home. But I often had to just give up. At home we had a phone from which we could only receive calls, so when the Sisters in Rome wanted to hear from us, they had to do the calling. For us to make a phone call, we had to use a card at pay phones.

I was often in trouble with the computer. I knew little. Sometimes I would open one, two, three, four new files and do not know how to close them. I was reduced to writing on a page just three centimeters high while I had all the other windows open. I kept asking Sister Amelia to pray so that I wouldn't wipe out everything. When they called me from Rome, I asked for advice, and the poor women didn't know how to make me understand. Of course I lost the pieces I had written. On rare occasions I found them somewhere else. It was unnecessary for the Sister in Rome to tell me to "Save" because I did not understand what "save a file" meant. The lessons that I had received before leaving were few, and on top of that I was not a good learner.

The advantage of living on our own brought with it self-management of everything: cleaning the house, prayer, food. At least we could bathe more often because the water was hot, and we were free to go around the city, to go to Mass in a small nearby church run by Italian Sisters. The latter, however, after a first friendly approach, looked at us without much sympathy. They saw us as possible competition, a threat to their territory. At that point, I had to tell them openly that we were not in Romania to found a House. We were there only in passing. This did bother us a little because we could see the difference between the Romanian Sisters who were hospitable and pressured us to remain in Romania, and the several Italian congregations that instead of encouraging us, made us understand that they were already there. After doing a little research we learned that after the fall of the regime, about sixty Italian religious congregations arrived in Romania, as well as others of different nationalities. It was obvious that they were looking for vocations and did not take kindly to those who might compete with them.

Our way of thinking was different. To start a foundation, the place had to offer the possibility of evangelization, or it had to respond to compelling needs. This we'd been taught by our founders. As a result, of course, we might get new vocations, young missionaries, but this should not be the priority. We talked at length about this with a Spanish Sister, a former Superior General of her Congregation. She, too, was staying with friends, visiting Romania for a period of rest after the end of her term. She understood the situation as we did, and together we thought of founding an inter-cultural and inter-religious center to find channels of communication with the Orthodox Church. Uunfortunately, we could not realize our project because at that point, neither she nor I had decision-making power in our respective Congregations.

The Romanian Sister friends helped us get to know Romania, taking us to places where they had some connection, a religious Community or a Sister in their Congregation or a priest who was their friend. We visited several cities, from east to west, north to south. I particularly remember the visit to Alba Iulia, where we were hosted by a Sister of the Congregation who lived alone, waiting to get into the Community. Right about that time, right there in that city, a big demonstration was organized in support of the newly elected President. In November of 1996 the parliamentary and presidential elections had seen the emergence of the opposition, united in the Democratic Convention and in the Social-Democratic Union. Emil Constantinescu, former rector of the University of Bucharest, was elected president. The town square was packed with enthusiastic people.

The Sisters wanted us to participate in this great moment, which for Romania represented the beginning of a new era. All the governments in power since Christmas of 1989, after the fall of Ceausescu, had disappointed people. With each new government, too many who had participated in the communist governments remained in office. Now, although the nation had passed through one crisis after another, people were full of hope. The plaza was alive with an atmosphere of celebration and joy that had never been known before.

After Alba Iulia, we went to Moldova, where there was the house of a nun who was always with us, Sister Margareta. She was a dear religious, young and kind. Her Father was an Eastern Catholic priest and had been in prison. He received us with great dignity and affection. Before we left, he placed in my hand a roll of paper. When I opened it, I saw a large number of banknotes, old and tattered but still valid. It really was the "widower's mite."

On another trip, accompanied by another young Sister, she took us to her house for a few days. But first she took us to the city of Oradea, on the border with Hungary. The home of this Sister, Sister Emilia, was large and comfortable, though Sister Amelia did not understand why all the houses were full of carpets. There was a large carpet on the floor of every room, and then several smaller rugs on top of one another. I thought that the little ones must be easier to wash or beat, which would be necessary because mud was often tracked in. In winter it would be sleet mixed with dirt. In this house we enjoyed affectionate and friendly hospitality. Every two hours they made us a substantial snack of tea, biscuits and homemade cakes. We ate something every time. We saw Sister Emilia eat with such gusto that it was a pleasure to watch her. Certainly in her convent she must have gone hungry.

In Oradea, where we arrived a few days later, always traveling by train, the Sisters knew a very good bishop who helped them a lot. In fact, the new congregation, not having official approval, could only be authorized by a bishop who declared it anchored in his diocese. This bishop was later cured of a serious illness in our clinic in Rome. In Oradea, Romanian nuns had been bequeathed a house by a wealthy Swiss gentleman but, at the time, they were unable to live there and take possession of it as Hungary claimed ownership. It was claimed that the house was in Hungarian territory. This dispute on the border between Hungary and Romania was very old and perhaps still exists today.

We went to visit the city of Cluj, where the seminary was. The Superior and master was a young priest. They told us that in the Eastern Catholic Church, if a priest decides to get married, he has to do it before being ordained, and to aspire to the office of bishop, he had to remain celibate. This was all very interesting to us, and there was no end to our questions. We ate with the students, who were many, and we were guests at

Parenthetical Pause

the home of a Sister who worked as a professor at the seminary and held other small jobs. To supplement their meager income, Sisters often spent the nights assisting the ill and elderly.

Another trip that really pleased us was on the opposite side from Oradea—Constanta, on the Black Sea. Since it was almost winter, we could not appreciate the beauty of the coast, which is so famous for its beaches. The weather wasn't bad, but there was little sun, and the sky was a bit gray. The sea, however, was pale blue! We were hosted by a family whose daughter was a candidate of the Congregation of our Sister friends. People were friendly everywhere, and I was surprised to meet so many people who spoke Italian. After a few weeks of lessons taught by a very kind Sister, we gave up because we didn't see any urgent need to learn the Romanian language.

Other important visits were in the mountains of Transylvania. The Sisters wanted to show us a parish where, if we wanted, we could found a mission. There was a large parish house, and the pastor would have been happy to have Sisters to help him. Of course we just listened and looked around. The house was really big, with high ceilings and a chill that cut to the bone. The pastor, a young married priest, a tradition of the Eastern Catholic Church, was living with his wife and a child in a large room that could be heated with a wood stove. There they ate, slept, and cooked. The rest of the house was cold. The priest explained that the living conditions made it difficult to support his family and the parish, but he hoped in time to have help to improve the state of the house. It had been long abandoned after being confiscated by the communists, like all properties of the Catholic Church, and it was now in poor condition. The return of these assets was a topic that in those months was a contentious issue between the Church and the new government. But the issue was still in its infancy. The scenery was beautiful, with small houses scattered here and there in the woods. We could only see the smoke coming from the chimneys. All around the mountains were already covered in the first snow. It looked like a creche.

We visited other cities, but the brevity of our stays in each does not allow me to remember anything in particular. Generally the Sisters, our friends, didn't take us to visit castles—how I wanted to see Dracula's castle!—or museums or historic buildings, but they took us to religious places and had us meet people who might be useful in our supposed missionary research. We visited many monasteries, some truly beautiful, especially the courtyards and churches, but we did feel the condition of life of the habitants: hard work in the fields harvesting vegetables and fruit, then loading everything onto wagons and selling it all at the market. All this was done by the Sisters. At home they prepared canned goods for sale. Often during the holidays they had to host priests with their wives, children and relatives in tow, feeding them and serving them like princes. One of the young Sisters, a candidate in Bucharest at our friends' Congregation, said that she had entered a monastery to pray, but prayer was the last thing she had time for. Work occupied her entire day. So she chose to leave and enter the Congregation of Sister Maddalena.

So the days passed. Winter was getting hard, but it was a dry cold that we didn't see coming right away. We were amazed that everybody already had their head and ears covered and wore winter clothes.

In Bucharest the Sisters made us aware of various situations concerning children, of which so much was spoken in Italy. It was said that in Romania, during the dictatorship, there was a triage among children who were born healthy and those deemed unsuitable for the nation. The latter were kept in dilapidated structures where they grew up in poor conditions, without medical care, malnourished and with no family life. We visited a hospital where international medical teams were already working for the recuperation of these children. People who came into contact with this reality told us of terrible experiences. An Italian journalist, Mino Damato, who died in July 2010, started a foundation, Children in Emergency, for children with AIDS in Romania. He adopted a sick child whom he loved very much and took to specialists for treatment. We knew that little girl and many others that he helped through his foundation. It seems that the death of the little girl struck the journalist deeply.

Of course, seeing so many things that could be done to

save these children, many of whom had congenital and physical abnormalities, my brain developed projects, opportunities, partnerships, and various strategies. But of course I had to come to terms with my condition as a powerless Sister. After all, I remember in such moments, when I accepted the position of General Superior, the only positive reason for accepting it that I could think of was to be able to decide some missionary initiatives. Now the good Lord was asking me only to make proposals and then let others make the decisions. This wasn't really a problem because, even when I had some power, there were always so many concrete situations to contend with. I knew that not everything could be done.

But the time of our stay came to an end. It was late December. One morning we woke up to rather deep snow. Then we realized that we were not dressed for winter, that our wardrobe was thin, our shoes unsuitable, and we were not used to walking on snow. If it had just fallen, it was soft and pleasant. But in the following days, as it froze on the roads, if covered in new snow, it was the cause of dangerous slipping. Mother Magdalene came to see how we were. She noticed that the propane bottle was empty and it was taking too long to get it refilled. She looked in the shed and saw that the firewood was almost gone. She looked in the refrigerator. It was almost empty. In an hour she was back, taking care of everything. Such was the incredible vitality of this Sister. She drove around in a little pickup and visited all her Sisters, the Foundations, the Houses, and she thought of

Parenthetical Pause

everything. She wanted to know how our stay in Romania had gone. We recounted our impressions and asked her to pray for our Congregation. She confessed that she suffered a lot from the hostile behavior of the local Church. She almost preferred the persecution and imprisonment because in that situation, at least she knew what the problem was and she could see the face of her enemies. Now, however, she did not understand the hesitation of the priests who had lived with her during that time of persecution and grace. We assured her of our prayers and our help if it was needed.

I could understand the concerns of the local Church, which did not want to be seen as superficially endorsing all the miracles that were attributed to the seer. It was said that she had foreseen the terrible situation that Romania would go through and that she was the center of extraordinary events. I also understood that loyalty to friendship that develops in difficult times is not always easy to sustain in normal times.

Christmas came. We expected that the Sisters would invite us to lunch that day, but they didn't. I think they were to celebrate it later, as they do in the Eastern Church. Anyway, we went to Mass at the cathedral, and we wanted to find a good restaurant, but we failed. We ate at home, very little, because we didn't want to buy more food since the next day, December 26, we had to return to Italy. Sister Amelia looked at me with irony and reproach: "Eh! Today is Christmas! Can't we have something better to eat?" But she ate very little, and I complained because

To the Ends of the Earth

I was always forced to finish the leftovers. But the company of Sister Amelia was excellent. We were very different in the way we thought and felt, but she was the best of friends. She put up with me and seconded my impossible dreams. It was a good experience.

We left the next day. The Romanian Sisters accompanied us to the airport, pleading with us to assure them that we would come back to found an institution.

They are still waiting.

15

Return to Missionary Life

In Rome I went to live at the Provincial House. I found the environment there not very agreeable, perhaps because of the transition it was going through. The Sisters who had arrived were changing roles. Maybe they weren't too happy about this. At the same time, the Provincial Mother's term was coming to an end, and she was committed to leaving everything in order. My presence might have been one cause of the confusion. These difficulties provoked a strange feeling. Was it possible they just didn't know what to do with a former General Superior? Anyway, I tried to calmly blend in with the environment. It was true that I didn't know the Italian Province very well, arriving after ten years of living abroad and another twelve years in the General

Curia, which can be considered kind of foreign. And it was true that now the Italian Sisters didn't recognize me as a member of the Province. But this lack of recognition constituted only a marginal factor. Perhaps the problem was something else. But my radical idealism prevented me from looking clearly at reality.

There were also two Sisters who came from another Province of the Institute who were also a little uncomfortable in that environment. Without meaning to be, it seemed unwelcoming.

I kept myself busy doing various things. For missionaries, work is always at hand. I gave a long report on living in Romania and sent it to the Mother General, who listened with interest. But I could see she had other ideas and other thoughts she intended to give a better hearing. Meanwhile, in early 1997, we celebrated an assembly of discernment to probe the opinion of Sisters on the appointment of the new Provincial Superior.

One day—I don't know if it was Easter time or the Feast of the Sacred Heart in June— the Sisters were gathered on via Sicilia near the Senior Rest Home. We were having a party. There was a bit of confusion, but the Mother General called me aside and, in a corner of the room full of Sisters and guests, asked me if I wanted to accept the office of Provincial Superior. To which I protested: "But how? Tell me, right here, right now, tell me!" But it was useless. She had already decided. She backed up her request by noting that the Sisters had given their opinions, etc. The new General Superior was not one of many pleasantries. She took my momentary protest as agreement. I had to accept.

As of the next day, everything changed. I set myself to looking for a place where I could live in peace and with a degree of autonomy, someplace separate from the Provincial Community, a place that could be considered an office and as a place to welcome Sisters who were passing through. I found an apartment on the Via Tiburtina. There I organized a Community for Sisters who came from abroad. There they could feel more free. We set up a little chapel that was really charming. The Sisters went out every day to attend their courses of study while I, when necessary, went to the Provincial House to deal with current business, unless I was traveling to the various Provincial communities and projects.

Usually deskwork took place at home, even though coming and going wasn't too hard. My life was like that of many people, going to work in the morning and returning in the evening. So I, too, was on Tiburtina Bridge, which was always so clogged that the bus took twenty minutes to cross it. Every morning I left the house to go to Mass in the parish, a parish adapted temporarily (for twenty years) in a garage waiting for permission to build at a nearby location. Often, however, I went to Mass at the basilica of San Lorenzo, which was two stops from my house. A few kilometers from my new Community was the Gordian Community, whose Mother Superior, Sister Emidia, followed us with affection and took care that we never lacked any necessities. She often sent someone to supply us with vegetables, fruit, or detergents. Sister Emidia's kindness was well known.

One of the things that bothered me a bit was managing the house, doing the shopping and cooking. The two Sisters who were with me were out all day, though they helped me with everything and kept the house clean as a mirror. But now I was used to making a virtue of necessity, and that situation seemed the most common thing in the world. Another minor issue was my relationship with the landlady. The apartment was rented for four years. She was a widow, still very young, who lived with her only son off the rent of various apartments. She called me almost every week for news, to ask pointless questions such as whether the gas meter had been read or to tell me how to open the shutter of the kitchen, or to remind me that the condominium meeting was scheduled for that day, etc. Sometimes she kept me on the phone for forty minutes to comment on all the events of her life, stealing valuable time. Eventually I resigned myself, considering the situation a little penance.

This new arrangement also had the goal of creating an alternative Community that would change our usual monastic ways, which in my opinion were making our lives a little rigid. But the solution was little understood and not really accepted. For me, however, this was part of religious life, and I continued on my way.

That first year went well as I became aware of my new

Return to Missionary Life

role as head of the Italian Province. The Great Jubilee of the year 2000 loomed on the ecclesiastical horizon. And in our Congregation, the 150th anniversary of the birth of our Founder, St. Frances Cabrini, was approaching, as was the centenary of her proclamation as Heavenly Patron of Emigrants. These two events involved me full time and were the cause of many headaches and much satisfaction. The headaches were many because of my busy schedule. I had to deal with my ordinary work as Provincial Superior, and I also had to handle the programming of these two events, which demanded a lot of cultural and spiritual effort. A Provincial Superior has an apostolic role but also an administrative and institutional role which involves a network of activities relating to projects as well as religious life. Although the projects have their own management and there are other people to carry them out, there is the charismatic and apostolic spirit to be kept alive through committees, visits, relationships, and periodic evaluations. Even more time-consuming is the management of the Communities and the relationship with the individual Sisters, which takes most of the time of a Provincial Superior. Also very difficult is the constant contact with the General Superior, who coordinates activities and decisions at the international level, whereas the Provincial Superiors are always involved, even with foreign travel and intense preparation in international meetings.

The priority that we had chosen for the Italian Province was an adequate preparation for the Jubilee of 2000. This event included the hosting of various groups from the world of Cabrini - and a celebration to accentuate the link with training in the Cabrini Missionary Identity. We organized an International Conference - in collaboration with the Pontifical Council for Migration - at the Synod Hall at the Vatican, an exhibition on emigration yesterday and today, a concert, and various other initiatives to bring out the message of St. Frances Cabrini. We worked hard at all levels. We were able to count on good cooperation from the Sisters, a bit less from the General Curia, which was busy on other more complex and demanding fronts. In addition, perhaps the Mother General did not want to give too much importance to our institutional culture because often the cultural dimension is seen as mundane, and anything that is not closely inherent to evangelization is little appreciated. This is a defect that we have been carrying for years.

One person who really helped us carry out many of these activities was Lucetta Scaraffia, who became the Institute's cultural consultant. She put us in touch with people and institutions that were able to help us pull off the various events. She made her house available for meetings with the people we had to meet, wrote articles for us, and advised us in various ways. Really I do not know how to thank her today. Of course, the hardest thing was to find the money to fund the scheduled events, money that ultimately came through the cooperation of our projects and Communities.

I must say that ideas without money become a real reason

of stress. To solicit funds I wrote a few hundred letters and received only a few vague answers. In the end, in the good Cabrinian way, I wrote to the leaders of our Italian projects and communities, who helped immediately. This confirmed to me once again that, as Mother Cabrini taught us, we should not expect much from our work and our sacrifices.

The preparation for the Jubilee entailed meetings, retreats, arrangement of subsidies, and even a newsletter to connect everyone in the spiritual preparation for the Jubilee. Also we welcomed many people from abroad and invited the Lay Cabrini Missionaries from Argentina to Rome to participate in the Jubilee. The organization work was heavy. We had to contact people, write, call, roll out programs and expect a thousand disappointments because the guests at various events often refused (perhaps an event was not considered prestigious enough or was financially difficult), so we had to start over from the beginning. We did not lack unexpected suffering.

One day I was in a meeting at Mrs. Lucetta's house. She was hosting us to schedule an exhibition about St. Frances Cabrini and emigration. It seemed interesting and involved the need to get free space in a train station in Rome. There we would set up the exhibition of photographs, objects, texts, music and so on. We were very happy with the idea. We contacted experts and were able to produce a beautiful and original exhibition. As we talked—as usual, we were perplexed on how to get funding—I got a phone call from the Provincial House. One of our Assistants

To the Ends of the Earth

General, a member of the General Council, had died of a heart attack. I was breathless. I mentioned it only to Lucetta and then ran out to visit the Mother General. She was devastated. The Sister was 58 years old and was a great missionary. She had been in Africa for twenty-five years. She was a wonderful person who had helped us a lot and had committed herself to accompanying the opening of a new missionary Community in Ethiopia—a decision made in the spirit of the Jubilee Year. At that moment, which was quite difficult for the Congregation, the Sister that God had called would be especially missed. In fact, despite the enthusiasm and vitality that our Institute showed, it was not uncommon that we had to struggle with the difficulties of projects, especially hospitals, schools and large institutions, which could no longer be sustained.

The death of missionary Sisters who were still on the field, in the middle of work, and the lack of vocations hit us especially hard and frustrated our desire to launch new initiatives. The life of a religious institute is always challenged by difficult situations of all kinds. But sometimes it seems that we can continue only by appealing to a greater hope, striving to understand that, whatever happens, God is walking with us.

The death of our Sister struck at the heart of the Institute, and it overshadowed all the cultural initiatives we were planning. We couldn't proceed with much enthusiasm because it seemed a contradiction in this time of grief. But I understood that, just as we learned in our religious vocation, life had to go on. Even when family members die, we often have to fight off our tears because certain commitments cannot be neglected. So it was for my brother's death, which occurred just as I was at a meeting in Milan. When I went to the funeral in Bologna, I burst into tears. Other relatives were amazed that a nun, who according to them is always in contact with Heaven, was crying so much. People often do not understand these things.

The consequence of this death was that I had to dedicate myself to doing even more and, with the help of some very good Sister collaborators, especially Sister Rachele, we managed to continue organizing the exhibition and the many other activities related to it. In fact, though we failed to have the exhibition set up in a hall of the terminal railway station or any important station in Rome, we managed to make it a mobile exhibition in a two-car tram, which for a month went around to the main squares of Rome. It was a very successful initiative! People entered the streetcar from the rear, visited the exhibition displayed on both sides of the car, with a spotlight system that would display emigration of the past on one side, and today's emigration on the other, with captions and music. At the driver's seat, there was a screen showing films about emigration. At the center of the car, in a display case, there were displays of artifacts and memories of the missionary life of Mother Cabrini. After visiting the exhibition, diverse groups of immigrants often gathered around and sang songs from their homelands.

We completed the preparation and implementation of a

conference to be held in the Vatican, in the Synod Hall, which was followed by a beautiful concert with José Carreras in the church of Santa Maria of the Angels. That same year we prepared a Cabrini agenda to be distributed as a tribute, with notes and memories of the Congregation.

I must admit, to tell it that way, it all seems rather easy, but it was all pretty complicated. For one thing, the agency that had to send invitations sent them very late, so many came only when the event was over. To make up for it we had to make hundreds of phone calls at the last minute.

I remember one little episode from those occasions—the story of Sister Rachele's pen. She was the Provincial Secretary, the same who was trying to deal with all the obstacles that we came across. Sister Rachele had tried to get the Synod Hall for free, but it seemed that we'd have to pay something. After many comings and goings and commitments to sign, at the last contact with the director who ran the Hall, Sister Rachele left a pen of some value there on his table. The pen had been given to her and was customized with the words "Sister Rachele." Perhaps the manager had already agreed to give us the room for free, even though it hadn't been stated, but Sister Rachel decided not to claim her pen and not to reopen the issue that had ended in our favor. "It's best to let sleeping dogs lie," she said, giving up her pen.

The first three years as Provincial Superior passed quickly through travel, meetings, schedules, visits, pleasant and difficult relationships, hopes and some disappointments. I must say, having to go from place to place, trips were often enhanced by the fact that Sister Rachele, an excellent driver, accompanied me, giving me the luxury of admiring the beautiful landscapes Italian roads offered us, even on routes as boring as the A1 motorway. The long rows of flowering trees during the spring, traveling from Milan to Bologna, near Modena and Parma, were unforgettable. You cannot imagine how joyful those flowers looked after seeing the same landscape shrouded in the gray mist of winter. I cannot forget the long stretches of sunflowers that bloom in the summer months, their yellow glowing across the landscape, or the red of poppies when spring is approaching. Nor can I forget the autumn color of the trees of the Pollino mountains as we navigated the endless Salerno-Reggio Calabria highway and then, when the coast of Calabria came into sight, the beautiful sparkling water of a sea more blue than you can imagine. Or the beauty of Sicily in spring and summer when the walls, the guardrails, the roofs of houses, and even ugly buildings are covered with bougainvillea, geraniums, and oleander. And in autumn the yellow-red prickly pears on the bulging plants, an almost majestic beauty. What is impressive is the light that illuminates everything and forgives the ugliness of concrete.

On one of those trips to the south of Italy, for long stretches, every few hundred meters you could see written on a sign, or a section of wall, or the wall of a home: "God exists." Who knows who enjoyed writing that, with the same uncertain calligraphy, for several kilometers. I saw it written for a number of years. I don't know if it's still there. Apart from the ingenuity, he was reaffirming that God is really there. Otherwise, how could we recount so many things that have given our life great meaning?

I was also gratified by another episode. During a trip to Brazil for an international meeting, the Mother General, as usual, called me aside for a few minutes and asked if we in Italy were willing to host an International Novitiate, whether we could accommodate young aspirants to religious life, young women from some Latin American countries, the United States and one from Russia, all of which belonged to our Province. It was a significant commitment because it meant dedicating a house to the Novitiate, establishing programs for their preparation, organizing many things that for many years had been done by other Provinces. For me it was very good news, but I had to hear the opinion of the other Sisters of the Provincial Council, those involved in training and taking all the bureaucratic steps needed to make an important decision. But the Mother General had already thought to ease up on the network of internal bureaucracy, so I went back to Italy with this new commitment, which involved a lot of organization.

The arrival of young people of various nationalities in the Italian Province brought a breath of fresh air, and for me the joy of being able to convey the story of Mother Cabrini and the Institute to novices who were young and very interested. Their enthusiasm infected many other Sisters who didn't think it was fair that young people who had so few years of religious life already knew our history and our charism more deeply than the others. So we organized various courses, lasting two years. Almost all the Sisters of the Province attended. The courses were held in stages of one or more weeks each year, with trips and pilgrimages that helped us to live the spirit of St. Frances Cabrini. Along with the preparation for the Jubilee 2000, the continuing education program helped create more harmony among the Sisters. I realized that every ideal must be constantly revived, not only with the mission, prayer, and the sacrifices of every day, but also by reviving our personal and institutional history in order to discover the path of God, what He does in spite of us, in spite of the many mistakes we make. It is He, God, who shines light on what we do in darkness.

Also in 2000 the first hundred years of the Mission of Turin were celebrated. My affection for this house, which was my first apostolic experience, from approximately 1961 to 1968, prompted me to devote some extra effort to the centenary. I was so pleased to immerse myself in the history of the foundation. I wanted to pull together all the information we had into a book.

For research I was able to use archives at the Mission of Turin, which was linked to the San Raffaele Cimena Mission in the hills a few kilometers from the town. Sisters in ill health went there to conclude their missionary life. Some were over a hundred years old. What moved me was to find in the archives

213

there the stories of many missionary Sisters who had died very young but died with the certainty that their lives were being donated to a cause. Though very young, they already felt themselves part of a missionary fate, that of the Congregation they had embraced. They believed that their suffering and prayers were part of a labor willed by God.

The archives hold a beautiful testimony from the doctor of that time, Dr. Vinardi, a highly educated man who was very involved with the spiritual experience of those Sisters. He stayed on for over ten years. He wrote:

> I remember with nostalgia so many beautiful and luminous figures of holy Sisters for whom, with true pain, speaking humanly and with human feeling, I had to care for and for the last time to pass my hand on their cold foreheads and eyes dead to earthy light [...], and how many times in my heart I thought that new and pure gems were added to the great procession of the bright celestial figure of Mother Frances Xavier Cabrini. And I don't mean to exaggerate, but I am convinced, having seen, to my great consolation, such beautiful and seraphic souls pass from their Institute to the heaven, souls that had little to envy of St. Therese of the Child Jesus.

Also preserved in the archives is a beautiful letter from a priest, the confessor of the Community for many years.

For me, writing that book was like taking a long course of Spiritual Exercises. Even if I could only write for a few hours,

Return to Missionary Life

or on some weekends when I could retreat to rest in Rieti, I was struck by the high spirituality that sustained those Sisters. Sometimes their experience caused me great suffering and even an inner struggle. I wondered constantly why suffering should be part of the Christian life.

I felt also felt an intense admiration for them. In that book I wrote:

> This period of the House of St. Raphael is marked by the heroism of the first Sisters, those who were sent because they were sick, and those who were sent to treat their Sisters. The story of those early days is a dramatic as well as a powerful witness. Between 1900 and 1930, 26 Sisters died there, most of them very young. We remember them as having the great spirit of prayer, the very strong sense of belonging to the Institute, the ability to suffer and to offer their sufferings. This is an unlikely root of Cabrini spirituality. Sisters, for the most passionate of missionary life, were taught about the sacrifices of the early days of the Congregation and the spirit of total sacrifice to God. Maybe a few years after entering the religious life—some were novices— they were forced to accept illness, to endure it and to see it progress without hope. It is impressive that, even in their serious condition, they wanted to live the life of community, prayer, work, and the sacrifices that this entailed. And when this was not possible, they prepared themselves to await death with religious dignity that is impressive today, but also with great faith, knowing

that that death, or that suffering, could be a sacrifice of atonement for the Kingdom of God, for the Church, for the salvation of others. This characteristic, inherent in the spirit of the Congregation named the Sacred Heart of Jesus in the nineteenth century, was in some way reinterpreted by Mother Cabrini, who, while retaining all the mystical interior, pursued her missions in a new and effective way. Everything you do has meaning if it is for the glory of God, and everything must be offered—not only the suffering, prayer and sacrifice, but also the work, the effort, the disappointment, the inner sacrifice of their own ideas and expectations. They are all things to sacrifice, the value of which is purified by love. So the mission, or whatever you do to proclaim the Gospel of Jesus Christ, has the value of atonement. Then, when the suffering, pain, death—sometimes arriving early—everything, falls into that salvationist process of mission that makes us partakers of the passion of Jesus and of his death, but also the passion of the world and of its sufferings. United with Christ, everything is redeemed.

In those first Sisters, who perhaps had never studied theology, one perceives a deep mystical insight that was the inner strength of the apostolic work first of Mother Cabrini, and then of her Institute. Of those Sisters one remembers above all their moments of illness and pain, even though they had also been good missionaries.[1]

---

1 Maria Barbagallo, *100 Anni di Missione, Le Missionarie di Madre Cabrini a Torino*, Gribaudi, Milano 2000, pp. 43-44.

Return to Missionary Life

The centenary was celebrated by an exhibition about the apostolic experience of Turin and by a very beautiful theater piece about Mother Cabrini, presented in a new theater space inaugurated in that centenary year.

Throughout 2000 we were much occupied also with the Codogno House, the first house founded by Mother Cabrini, reorganizing the museum; with the birthplace of Sant'Angelo Lodigiano, which required structural changes; and with many other things that aimed to make the reception of the pilgrims more pleasant. I often felt guilty about the hard work, which involved a continuous reorganization of our Houses, especially those in which feasts were being celebrated. Also in Rome, the church on via Sicilia, a sacred place for many of our celebrations, was restored for the occasion and outfitted with new windows. There we celebrated the fiftieth anniversary of the religious life of the Mother General, which we wanted to celebrate with all the Sisters of the Institute who shared the same anniversary.

I remember with great satisfaction that on this occasion I wanted a children's choir of "white voices" to be organized from our Italian schools. After the many difficulties that this event involved—it was certainly not easy to overcome resistance coming from everywhere—I have to confess that the day these children came to sing in the church of the Redeemer was like being in paradise—a beautifully performed *Discite e Me (Learn from Me)*, which was very famous in the Institute but had not been sung for thirty years, and I think that it was composed by

217

a Sister. They also sang the Ave Maria Pachner with the words of Carducci, which I had never heard sung so well. I think I'm the only one to remember with joy the moment, perhaps for the struggle that I needed to achieve it. Of course, non-combatants cannot enjoy a victory.

I remember from that celebration with pleasure the gift that my Community arranged for the Mother General. The two Brazilian Sisters who were with me asked, very worried, what they could give to the Mother General. They were very expert, one to embroider in cross-stitch and the other to make lace. They prepared fifty embroidered doilies trimmed with lace. Starched and closed up by a golden string, they became little candy sacks, a splendid display. We put them all together in a basket covered with a large embroidered doily. It was really beautiful. The Sisters who created such a wonderful thing could hardly believe how successful it turned out to be.

Thus ended the first three years of my term as Provincial Superior. I was then confirmed for three more years, until 2003.

Life went on at an increasingly intense pace. Now it was a time to make known to our young Sisters the beauties of our shrines, our works, our traditions. They renewed the liturgy— their songs to the sound of the guitar and their crystalline voices really enlivened our assemblies and Community. But even here there was no lack of sorrows, disappointments, doubts. We felt the beauty of young people but also their fragility, their fear of commitment forever, their suffering before a life that promised nothing but dissatisfaction.

The joy of religious professions celebrated in the Church of the Redeemer in Rome, in the end, made us forget the difficulties in completing the period of preparation for religious life. But even that was just the closing of a parenthesis. The young women, their training period concluded, one by one returned to their countries of origin. Some remained for some years, but then were recalled by the Sisters of their province.

The missionary life involves these rapid movements of people and mission. Sometimes the intense pace brings about the loss of the deep bonds that have been woven among people, often with difficulty. One is always about to leave a place or people to venture into new experiences and be of service in a new situation. The heart of a missionary must be able to retain the inner structure of her existence without time taking away all the good and important things she lives for. For me, time seemed marked by an invisible clock which marked the calendar of trips, meetings, people I had to see, and the many problems that I had to try to solve, year after year, to achieve the objectives and assess whether it was necessary to change them and start again.

The spaces of silence and prayer, which fortunately begin and end the day, continually recall the meaning that is given to each activity. For truly, delusions never fail, nor does the feeling that time passes inexorably and always seems shorter and shorter. Quasimodo is right to entitle one of his poems:

To the Ends of the Earth

"And suddenly it is evening."

For the Jubilee Year, in which the Church invites us to engage in repairing many forms of injustice, for the evil committed in the past by individuals, companies, and nations, our Congregation decided—besides opening a new missionary Community in Ethiopia—to start a service for the terminally ill. Thus was born the Hospice at the Columbus clinic in Milan, inaugurated in 2003. The Italian Province participated joyfully in this new initiative, for which previous attempts had been to no avail. Experience has confirmed the great human and Christian value of this work. It is a great moment of grace for many people, young and adult, of all social conditions, in the most dramatic moment of their lives, when God makes them understand the true values of existence. There is much pain, but it is also a moment of grace for other people, family and friends, so the experience of pain and death can glimpse the transcendent dimension of life.

For me, participating in the gestation of this initiative was particularly important. I entered in spite of myself, trying to understand a bit more the sense of moral and spiritual pain of those who consciously know they will die soon. Let me cite one of the many experiences that have been published in a pamphlet printed to celebrate the first five years of the Hospice:

> Ivan Lucchini went into hospice after having himself baptized. His godmother wrote a brief biography: Photographer, director, coordinator of

events related to the world of advertising and fashion. His parents, partisans and communists, decided not to baptize him. All his life Ivan was, perhaps, fundamentally convinced—as he confided only at the end—that he was unfortunate, pursued by bad luck, because he had not been baptized. Girls who, after illusions and promises, abandoned him; physical ailments and dissatisfactions with work: things normal and common, but for Ivan so important as to become almost a sickness.

So he moved to Greece, where the climate is milder, and the light and the sun make life more serene. Finally a girl appeared to be the right one for him. But after years, that story ended, too, and Ivan found himself again lonely and sad: a black swan.

Then came illness, and the thought of baptism reappeared in his heart. Friends and loved ones encouraged him and helped him to recognize that whisper, like a cry for help, a search for light and joy. Ivan is no longer alone. He is serene and calm. He chose, and his heart is quiet. Ivan has entered the light.

This and other experiences, gained by living a bit in that almost holy environment of Columbus in Milan, make you understand things you could not understand even from reading a thousand books.

The hardships that one faces in the missionary life have no material rewards, but there are many spiritual rewards. What comforts us, in the midst of conflicts that need to be addressed, is to know that we do not fight to achieve our particular objective but for a higher end, an end so lofty that we do not know the scope of it.

16

Obligatory Passages

The period after my second term as Provincial Superior was also difficult, but for different reasons. It was the same in that no one made decisions on where and how I would continue my missionary life. With that freedom, there was a period of my not knowing what to do. Then one of my birth sisters took seriously ill. Her illness progressed for several years, but at the end of 2003 and the first half of 2004, it got much worse—the rush to hospitals, the slight improvement followed by a more serious deterioration and, finally, in July, her death. This coming and going from hospitals and rehabilitation centers was stressful but it let me experience the goodness of people and their supportive friendship.

To the Ends of the Earth

I was touched by the care that my brother-in-law gave my sister. It was an intensive care, more than a paid professional nurse could provide. It was a little in his own way, but it was still admirable. Their two sons, in different ways, tried to be present, especially the younger, who was living in London and trying to take some extra vacation time mostly to stay with his mother. The other lived nearby but wasn't as useful in terms of assistance. I, meanwhile, was at a Gordian center on the outskirts of Rome, where I was working a little at the school and a little at the Community, but without real conviction because I was still waiting for something that hadn't yet happened. I don't know if it was excessive submission or for the lack of clarity of the situation. Perhaps both.

At that time, a young Sister accompanied me on the Stations of the Cross of my sister's illness and death. This nun, Sister M.M., had a special gift for helping people in the worst moment of life, when they are about to leave it. She had an extraordinary ability to speak with people who were sick, when she could, and when she couldn't, she put her therapeutic and spiritual insights at the service of the family. It was she who found a way to talk calmly with my sister's children. It was she who smoothed my visits with intimacy and understanding. When a Sister of her Community was dying she placed herself next to her bed and, whether the Sister heard them or not, whispered comforting words and prayers full of hope and confidence. It was a spiritual gift.

About the death of her father a few years before, Sister M.M.

Obligatory Passages

told me about her experience in a letter, from which I quote only a few parts. Her father had left her mother for another woman and had started another family. He maintained good relations with the first wife and especially with the children. Of course, this wound left many consequences in the children, but Sister M.M., as a good Christian, had always tried to mediate, more with her behavior than with words. The situation became more difficult when it came to going to the hospital and meeting the woman he had married after abandoning her mother, and also meeting the brothers with whom they had never had relationships. She won over the reluctance of his family. So, among other things, she wrote:

> The next day I went to the hospital with my aunt, who had me talk to the doctor. He told me the plain truth: Father had little time to live. They gave me permission to enter the intensive care unit to be alone with him. When I saw him, seeing how he suffered, I felt a great pain. I can still see his image: a tube in his mouth to breathe, a drip feed—he was a suffering Christ. He could not speak, but he always listened to me. I do not know where I found the courage, but I remember that I said: "Dad, it's time." My heart was pounding. I felt like crying. He responded by moving his head as if to say "no." He seemed to me like a child saying "no." But I continued to prepare him. "Dad, do not be afraid, Jesus is here with you, He loves you. I have forgiven you and in the name of my mother and my brothers I forgive you. God has forgiven you, you do

not owe anything to anyone, we have forgiven you. " He cried. I continued: "Jesus is waiting, He is here with you, do not be afraid. You have taught us to love him and believe in him. You have taught me many things that I have learned...." And I prayed the prayers he knew, the Our Father, the Hail Mary, the Salve Regina, and I kept telling him, "Do not be afraid, Jesus is merciful, he loves you." I left the intensive care unit in peace but with the anguish of knowing that at any moment God could take my Father. Only God gave me the strength to talk to him as I spoke.

I left the ICU in peace but anxious that at any time God could take my dad. Back home I told my mother and my brothers, "Dad is about to die."

The behavior of this Sister in the face of her father's death was an example for me, too.

During my stay at the school in Rome, taking advantage of the fact that it had just taken on a new principal, I tried to make some changes that seemed important. But I could not achieve any lasting change. A few months later, when I changed communities, everything went back to the way it had been. This issue of changes I made but which did not develop later was a continuing frustration that I had always suffered. On the one hand, I had to admit that perhaps the new idea did not always come at the right time or in any case was not something that could be understood by the people who were managing the situation. On the other hand, it is extremely difficult to "patch up an old piece with a new one," as Jesus says, more or less, in the Gospel. In our religious contexts, then, it is even more difficult because most people, including the laity who work with us, tend, like the Sister, to maintain the same patterns of behavior without real critical awareness.

It is people who come from outside who realize that the system, the mode of organization, the pedagogical approaches, the people who go on doing the same thing, are the cause of poor development of the project. The risk of failure blocks people and, for lack of patience and courage, they boycott new initiatives. So then failure comes and makes them right: "We told you so."

My age, my experience, my knowledge of situations, in general, has taught me not to make a tragedy. But I cannot deny that when I see the death of initiatives that were beginning to create a new mindset and generate new interests, it disconcerts me. Typically, the economic issue, which was always becoming more urgent and difficult, became dominant, so it was necessary to always make a budget for each project and analyze carefully whether there was money to carry it forward. It is a necessary mindset, undoubtedly, but one which, I maintain, should not be a priority. Our ideals, our history and our tradition, have they not taught us that we must have great confidence in Providence? Everyone agreed on this, but the facts then went in the opposite direction.

However, I am convinced that even with these problems,

the Kingdom of God will go forward. There is always someone who wants to make us understand that "we must seek first the Kingdom of God and His righteousness, and the rest will be given unto you."

In July 2004 they transferred me to Codogno, still without my knowing exactly why or what I had to do. The Sisters also welcomed me with questioning faces—*What did you come here to do now?* These situations of uncertainty are experienced with difficulty by the person who has to deal with them because they leave a strong feeling of being insignificant. Many Sisters have told me that they have also lived through moments in which—perhaps without malice—others show surprise and inability to understand that whoever has arrived there is in a state of great distress, and that you should do everything possible to alleviate it.

I did not feel as out of place as many may think, but given the lack of clarity, I had to go through this tunnel. For a few years I lived in a small apartment that we had set up, years before, for whatever came up or to accommodate people. The person was now me. We called the little house "Casa San Giuseppe," and it greeted me with love. It was the hen house of an old rustic house in Codogno and now was renovated. It was really charming. At the time, when it was being fixed up, Sister Emidia was overseeing it. She was a Sister who could make anything beautiful. She had an extraordinary talent for hospitality. She put love into everything under her care. She had outfitted the whole house with doilies on the bedside table and other tables, with curtains, pots and serving dishes, linens for the bedroom, and even a little library. We also made a small nook in the wall and set it up with a framework where we could hold the Blessed Sacraments, for the benefit of those who used the house for long retreats of solitary prayer. There was a kitchenette, and everyone helped me through that hybrid period in which, hoping to rest a little, I became part of the joy of being in the first house founded by St. Frances Cabrini. It was so rich with her memories, with her room and with the relic kept in the big church in Tabor, her heart.

The hope of rest faded away. Almost without realizing it, the Mother General stacked me up with work because our Congregation was preparing to celebrate the 125th anniversary. It was to be held in Codogno. As usual, I was called to handle them with poor Sister Rachel, who, in the meantime, had been transferred to Milan. I had to prepare an international course on the charism and history of the Institute, which was to take place soon. It completely absorbed me for seven weeks.

Between preparation and other activities, however, I had a bit of time. I wanted very much to write the story of our mission in China, from 1926 to 1951, so I plunged into the documentation kept in Codogno.

The experience was interesting because I had to study the history of China in order to understand what they were referring to in the hundreds of letters. I got a stiff neck from copying the letters that had been written by the Sisters who were missionaries there. Sister Rachel kindly gave me a computer program with which I could dictate letters without having to type them. The system worked, but then I had to read very carefully because the computer sometimes interpreted my voice wrong, so of course I had to correct everything. But the program helped me.

I was plunged into our Chinese mission in every sense as I studied the customs of the Chinese, their practices, the types of food, the wars and floods that occurred in that period, the persecutions that our Sisters suffered. I was helped a lot by the stories of some of the PIME (Pontifical Institute for Foreign Missions) missionaries in their memoirs, which described the same things the Sisters' letters were talking about. The Fathers were more organized in presenting places and the reasons for war. Their diaries were really beautiful.

Through these letters I felt myself there with the Sisters, to feel the humid heat that turned their black habits grey with the salt of their sweat, their trips between the Kashing and Shanghai missions, and the Honan and Kashing missions. And the diseases, the joys, the frustrations with the schools which they founded, schools where they could not talk about religion unless the pupils were of Christian families. I felt immersed in the problems of their community and in recognizing the difficulties with the relationships they went through. I admired their heroism in transcending all difficult situations and looking beyond to the true meaning of their missionary choice. In short,

Obligatory Passages

it seemed to me I was with them, sharing their fate, especially when they were first prisoners of the Japanese, then of the Chinese, then persecuted by the troops of Mao's enemies, and then by Mao's troops.

In short, it was a dramatic and beautiful epic, starred with emotional episodes, such as one involving three brigands. The Sisters were fleeing across the marshy rice fields in their long, black dresses. They asked one of the thieves to carry an older Sister on their shoulders because she was about to faint. For payment in cash, of course. Once they'd moved her, the robbers refused the money, saying: "Sisters, we are the prisoners who were confined in your House by the Japanese, and you brought us water and food in secret." Related as an example.

Faced with that experience, my situation of being in semi-exile passed into the background, even though it was an abnormal condition and at times many of our lay partners looked at me puzzled and asked for explanations. I answered that we were in a time of transition and so on. It was too hard to explain.

But there were many nuns, silent and unnoticed, who took care of me: the one who sent me virgin honey, knowing my ecological preferences; the one who sent me excellent homemade jams; the one who sent me Sicilian cookies; the ones who got me something that they knew I might possibly need; and the ones who came to console me with their innocent and affectionate interest, such as the young novice from Argentina who came by every day to ask me if she could do something for me. Actually I didn't lack anything important. Just I felt the strangeness of the situation.

The celebrations, the people coming and going, the parties, meetings, shows and conventions took place throughout 2004 and 2005. The events always saw me totally committed. It was nice to see so many people—Sisters from other parts of the world, everyone sharing with us the celebrations, memories, and especially the mission. They were constantly inviting me to their missions. They wanted me to teach courses on the charism, the history of our Institute, and other things. But I honestly thought that now was the time when I had to take care of something else. I didn't know what, but certainly God knew.

When it was all over, my situation in some way defined itself. Mother General had wanted to commemorate the 125th anniversary of the founding of our Congregation by realizing the dream of Mother Cabrini. She wanted to build a church where the Blessed Sacraments were shown all day long for perpetual adoration. Of course, the church was already there. It was built after her death, but Mother General was thinking about a little chapel supported by a small Community. For that initiative she consulted the Sisters of the entire Congregation, asking who would be willing to be part of this Community, for which the Mother General had prepared a small apartment within the complex of the House. Two permanent Sisters would be enough to form the new Community, and a third could be a guest from Italy or abroad who wanted to spend a few days or weeks or months in adoration and thanksgiving to the Lord. After all, there were always many missionaries who requested periods of spiritual rest. The Mother General chose two candidates: Sister Olga, from Argentina, and Sister Emidia, from the Community of Rome where she thought the Sister should step down and be replaced by another Sister. I was not among the candidates because they did not expect me to be a suitable person for that Community. Nor had I asked. After several attempts and discussions, we prepared a small chapel that could be accessed directly from the street so that the faithful outside could come and go freely.

Some months before 14 November 2005, the day of the Foundation—the day that was supposed to begin the experience—Sister Olga, after a brief and inexplicable illness, died, and Sister Emidia was afflicted by a very serious stroke that paralyzed her, forcing her into a wheelchair for the rest of her life, although, fortunately, it left her mind clear. General Superior heard comments that weren't exactly correct from Sisters. They were saying things like, "Perhaps the Lord does not wish ...." But the General Superior could not be swayed. "When I finish my term," she said, "I will be ready to come." That was how I offered to be part of the new Community, which in the meantime had found another volunteer and a Sister from Brazil. I moved to the new Community. Jesus was calling me to be a little closer to Him.

233

17

To Live on Mission, But...

Of course it took a little time for the new Community to find a balance. Not everyone agreed that this Community be formed at a place where there were already two. Nevertheless, we began the new experience.

There were three of us—an elderly Sister who came from Milan and wanted to dedicate the last years (or days) of her life exclusively to Jesus; and a Sister from Brazil who wanted to have a few months of spiritual rest; and me. We each had small roles in the Community. As usual, I took care of dinner. We had lunch together with another Community. We also had to organize Community life, but we quickly adjusted to the new rhythm. For the Adoration we took turns. It was especially nice to see people coming to the chapel to pray to Jesus, who was shown in the Blessed Sacrament and to ask for grace. It was an opportunity to get closer to people's pain. Later we put up a bulletin board on which people wrote the intentions of their prayers. It was amazing how young and old found hope only in God after trying many other ways. How many disappointments, how many worries and sufferings—disease, depression, broken families, young people and adults looking for work. Sister Emidia, who also came to Codogno, was the constant presence in the chapel from the opening day. She greeted almost everyone who entered. Thanks to her presence I could have someone in whom to confide in my small and big adventures. Sister Emidia was always a good friend.

I took care of the general things concerning the chapel, but a few hours a day, when I was not otherwise occupied, I spent before the Blessed Sacrament. The silent presence of God at times unsettled me, and I asked myself about my faith and my means of believing. God is really silent, an eloquent silence that creates a longing to know more, to better understand his mystery; but it is hard to enter into his mystery with intelligence or with words. We need the wisdom that comes from Him. So many times my only prayer was and is the Song of Solomon: "Give me Wisdom, the consort at your throne, and do not reject me from among your children [...] Send her forth from your holy heavens and from your glorious throne." (Wisdom of Solomon 9: 4, 10). This experience gave me the opportunity to think more,

To Live on Mission, But...

to think more about the Word of God, to establish connections between the Word and my life, to enter more deeply into myself. I often recited Psalm 139: "Lord, you have searched me and known me." And often too prayed more for others who asked for help constantly. Since then, this is my life, with periods of more or less intense presence.

In the afternoon, before closing the chapel, we celebrated the rosary and vespers with the people who happened to come from the area; it was very nice to share the prayer with everyone. Some people entered immediately into tune with Jesus and with us, and they will always be. With some of them we became really good friends. An elderly lady, a single, childless widow, was unfailingly there every afternoon and learned to pray the vespers with us like a religious expert. Others came occasionally and sang and prayed with us.

As the months went by, the devotees changed. Some were older people who could no longer leave their homes. Others needed to look after their grandchildren. Others got sick and they sent someone to ask us to pray. Others died. We missed their presence, but one knows that also Jesus as Sacrament must follow the pace of life of his worshippers. As the book of Ecclesiastes says: "There is a time to live and there is a time to die."

But the ones who came to pray always were the elderly Sisters who lived in a part of the House that we called "House of the Sacred Heart." They were missionary Sisters who, due to old age or illness, led a quieter life after spending fifty or sixty years or more on mission. They were always present, at least a few hours a day, and they are truly like living beacons. Among them are Sisters ninety or more years. Their presence, too, varies or decreases with either illness or death.

So even the death of a Sister was for me an experience that I was not used to. Yes, in our Communities, as in all families, there is always someone who dies. But in a Community of very old people, it is more common to experience the arrival of death. It comes to tell us that one day or the other, it will touch us, too. Some feel that this closeness to the elderly is a reason for depression or at least an uncomfortable experience. I must say that for me it is an experience of faith. Yes, I am very sorry when one of our Sisters leaves us, and I feel sorry for their mental and physical decline—Sisters we knew to be creative, intelligent, lively, and full of vitality in fulfilling their mission. I cannot hide a certain inner discomfort—my suffering. At the same time, when you can share their decline because their mental capacities allow, it is also a great witness of faith. One receives a lot of hope.

They await their Bridegroom, as they often say, to finally know him face to face, as one of our Sisters put it. They pray with perseverance. If they can read, they follow the events of our missionary life and that of the Church. They listen to the radio, watch religious programs on television. For as long as they can, they do little manual tasks. Sometimes they suffer loneliness

To Live on Mission, But...

that often touches a life that is about to end. Sometimes their character changes to become more taciturn. But they say the prayers that are asked of them. Priests who happen by ask them to pray for their parish. Relatives visit them and ask to pray for them. Our distant missionaries ask for prayers, and so do many people. When we see our Sister missionaries pass away one by one, it makes a great impression on us, but we feel their presence in another way. They are still here with us to share the only real life, the one that never ends.

My work on the history of the Missionaries in China went on. In my research I discovered many interesting things about my Congregation. So when Mother General told me to write the history of our Institute, I threw myself into it. Mother Lina Colombina was General Superior at the time, already in her second term. She was very wise and spiritual, passionate about the Archive of the Congregation that had to be reorganized and computerized, and very respectful of the written tradition. She had her own way of giving assignments. She never told you specifically, but she made you understand. "Now," she said. "I think we can start a history of the Institute of the Missionaries of the Sacred Heart."

I didn't have to be told twice. MSC is an organization that fascinates me. But perhaps she did not think it was a very demanding job. In any case, for me it was a big commitment. I continued to read, research, and put together Sisters' "Memories," which are somewhat like journals that all Sisters

239

are expected to keep while on mission. Memories and letters were the most authoritative sources for compiling a history. I copied into the computer thousands of letters and almost all the Memories that the Congregation keeps and which consist of a detailed description of the origin of all the Foundations initiated by Mother Cabrini. There are also written records from the years following the death of the founder—all the letters, reports, articles, newspapers and internal newsletters, all valuable documents that I learned to appreciate, even with a bit of fanaticism. It was a job that involved a lot of effort. It may have been the cause of various illnesses that I suffered for some time.

In the same way, the Mother General made me realize that the Cabrini Museum, which we had already rearranged a couple of times, always here in Codogno, wasn't done very well. It would have to be organized in a more rational way. It should be a real museum. Until that time, even though we had put a lot of effort into it, it was just a collection of memories, objects and documents about the Mother Cabrini, in no particular order and shown without much care. This also she made me realize, without directly giving me the assignment. It was going to take me a while to get myself organized. Each project I did I submitted to her scrutiny, and she looked at me puzzled, without telling me whether it was good or bad. But I could tell something from the look on her face. Eventually I realized that I had to get to work without much consultation and use other criteria. In

To Live on Mission, But...

2008 the 15th General Chapter of the Congregation would be celebrated in Codogno, in our Community house. It was to host some seventy people, including Sisters and lay people from all over the world, wherever there were Cabrini missions. So the real purpose of radically overhauling the museum was to present to the Congregation a well done museum.

This new commitment enabled me to choose excellent collaborators. First of all, an expert museologist, young and capable, intelligent and precise. She touched every document and every object with sacred respect. I exercised patience in a way I never imagined because of the slow tempo of her work, the long times off that she took for family commitments, the waits, and everything you can imagine. Several times we had to put off an inauguration program because we wouldn't be done in time. I was backed up by other collaborators—framers and restorers, window dressers, carpenters, painters, electricians. They were mostly young people who were very responsible in their craftsmanship. Working with them taught me many things about rationality, simplicity and perfection in exhibiting objects and in treatments and colors. And, as I said, they taught me about patience because the museum could not be designed all at once. It had to be designed by areas so that one sector harmonized with another. The colors couldn't conflict with each other. I was surprised at how good they were. You would have to know them and work with them to experience it. Meanwhile, as things dragged on, I had to continue a peaceful struggle—as peaceful as possible—with the Sisters.

You can imagine what it means to keep two or three spaces closed off with a sign that says "No access, being restored" and then open a half-ready corner and hear comments such as "What? That's all? And it took so long?" Lay people who passed by for other reasons or to go to Mass in the Sisters' chapel said, "But why didn't they use such-and-such a material, which is better and doesn't hold moisture?" Or: "This is going to be it? Who was advising you?" And so on. Every now and then the Mother General passed by and looked perplexed. But since my face was perhaps giving off signs of frustration that seemed to say, "Please don't you chime in…," in the end, she said nothing. The Provincial Mother was not one to encourage me so, poor thing, she didn't say anything to me, just listened to the comments of the Sisters—and who knows what they told her!

For the photographic section of the exhibit, we called another colleague who did the job much faster. Fortunately. The last act of this stressful epic had to do with with a graphic artist whom we called to prepare brochures and posters for the inauguration. Really good but stuffy and full of himself. Finally I had to give in to his tastes. I must admit that he was clever, but in my heart I kept telling myself, "I will not call you again."

Finally the major part of the work was complete. I thought the results were good. The inauguration took place while I was struggling with a number of ailments, especially with labyrinthitis, which restricted my freedom of movement

To Live on Mission, But...

because I risked falling down. Many times I had to walk looking straight in front of me without turning my head. For nearly two years these crises recurred without obvious reasons. And then also I suffered other health problems caused by advancing age.

And then there was the preparation of the General Chapter celebrated in Codogno. Although this wasn't up to me, I did a lot of work, traveled abroad even, documents to prepare, reports, and meetings. When there was something to write or some documents to compile, they always came to me. When they asked: "What do you do in Codogno?" I answered, "Everything nobody else wants to do." It was one aspect of our mission that no one can imagine.

I remember, when I was in Romania, the General Superior of the Sisters who hosted us, who had been elected for a few test years, wanted me to explain how to prepare a General Chapter. I explained in broad terms what was involved. After carefully listening to me, she said, "I'd rather die than do all that work." She exaggerated, of course, but the institutional aspect of a religious congregation is very complex. It takes as much love and faith as a mission. The organization isn't everything, but it's very important. Some missionary Sisters complain about this bureaucratic work. It requires a lot of energy, a lot of attention, a sense of the institution, love for the Congregation, and a global vision of missionary life. Sometimes it's hard to understand and make out the kingdom of God among the letters that are on your desk. We need His grace.

To the Ends of the Earth

The time of the General Chapter arrived. The first part of this International Assembly was to review the entire mission of the Congregation all over the world. It was the most beautiful part. You came to know extraordinary experiences, made possible thanks to new paths that missionaries create when they realize that the traditional pastoral is not working.

For example, one Sister, a missionary in Southern Africa, related that they had decided to leave that mission to travel to a place of more immediate emergency. But when they got together with the locals to leave the ongoing projects in their hands, they noticed a terrible situation. Hundreds of children were wandering here and there because their parents were dying or had already died of AIDS. The children themselves were infected. The Sisters had to open an orphanage. They remained there and reprogrammed their missionary activity around the prevention and treatment of a disease that no civil authorities were willing to even recognize.

Another Sister said that in Central America they had decided to take care of some abandoned children living in a center funded by a rich woman in the United States. The government had shut down the center because the same people who were entrusted with the children had abused them. Another Sister, engaged in vocation ministry, organized training sessions on Christian discernment for young people. When adults became aware of the work she was doing with young people, they also wanted to know how to make a discernment. So she welcomed

To Live on Mission, But...

people of any age.

Every event was presented with photographs, interviews, movies. The bureaucratic fatigue of preparing the Chapter served to celebrate the missionary life. I was not new to these things, but the missionary life in my view had changed, and now went on in a different way.

At the Chapter I presented the first volume of the History of the Institute of the Missionaries of the Sacred Heart. It started after the death of Mother Cabrini, going up to the 1950s. Three volumes. It was not a complete story, but a first version, to continue and complete with additional documentation. Sister Rachele had done a great job of polishing it up. She put it on "keylets," that is, pen-drives, so everyone could copy it. I later gave a copy to a missionary Sister in Russia who was not able to attend the Chapter. A few months later she sent me this letter:

> I write with feelings of appreciation and gratitude for the great and unexpected present you made for me when I came to Codogno to see you—the DVD and the pen drive containing the History of MSC. I'm still very moved because I could see and enjoy, only briefly for now, a little of the "History." I can not describe what emotion I felt when my hand clicked the index. I could not believe my eyes. Sometimes I burst with joy, saying to myself: "What a treat Sister Mary gave me! The History of the Institute to carry with me?" I do not know how to thank you. I will treasure this beautiful gift. I see this as a good reason and a great meaning to rekindle the gift that God gave me when he put me

in the Missionary Sisters of the Sacred Heart of Jesus. Yes, Sister Maria, in these years of my stay in Russia I have had a good chance to continue in my personal formation, the path of faith offered by our Constitutions and the General Chapters. Therefore in my "Personal Project" I will not lack the time to deepen the "History of the MSC." It's still missing the third part. I hope that will come to light. I am sure, as St. Paul says, that "He who begins a good work in thee, will perform it…" (St. Paul to the Philippians). I am grateful to the Sacred Heart of Jesus, who bestows His Spirit, illuminated in time to give the Institute a great legacy, the result certainly of prayer, work, sacrifice, offering, and gift. All for the MSC. and for the benefit of all grace. And with this my small, poor and humble mission, with this reading of the history of the MSC, is increasingly clear. Thanks again for this enrichment, because knowing the history allows us to create stronger bonds of belonging to the Institute, and each of us can help the Institute to achieve a deeper level of the charism to live it and so achieve the gift of ourselves in response to the call.

18

Fifty Years of Religious Life

Codogno is a town in the lower Po valley, in the province of Lodi. Its origin is very old. It's an ancient village that has resisted time, becoming a large town, unlike many other villages, which were absorbed into neighboring towns or have disappeared. The people are very private and quite closed to innovation and anything different, but they're educated and generally affluent. For fun, they go to Milan or Cremona or any other of the several cities not far away. It's not particularly interesting as a town, apart from the beautiful churches and their valuable frescoes, something common in Lombardy. And then there are the market days, which seem to revive the town's usual torpor. Its climate isn't too healthy—warm and humid in the summer, cold and wet in the winter, which lasts too long. In the spring, however, when the surrounding countryside blooms along with the garden roses of houses and beautiful villas, there is an air of festivity and color. In autumn the magnificent sycamore of the avenues take on gorgeous colors, but the color soon ends with the first rain and wind.

Here St. Frances Cabrini founded the first house of our religious Institute, in a battered old Franciscan monastery that she bought, which for her was the theological location of all her apostolic and missionary action. I arrived there in 2004, after the events that I have previously described and where I have already done some of my new mission. Of course, when I leave Codogno and go to Milan or Rome, it's like being in another world, but that's small town life.

After the first months away, I begin to see the positive side of many things. For example, the people. Despite the close-mindedness that they show, when they establish a relationship without any self-interest, they are friendly and cooperative. I found good people, even some precious friends who have always been willing to do me a favor. As craftsmen, they are good, honest and intelligent. The landscape: when you go a little outside of town, you see the classic landscape of the River Po plain—flat, with large expanses of land sown with wheat, corn or forage. But when you reach the River Adda and the River Po, and venture into one of the few remaining forests, you feel the unmistakable charm of the fog, the color of the sky, the

Fifty Years of Religious Life

long rows of poplars that mark the boundaries of properties, the many castles—some well preserved, others somewhat derelict—which belonged to one feudal family or another. The farmhouses, almost all restored, are in large buildings a little reminiscent of the film *The Tree of Wooden Clogs*, a little of the landscapes described by Alessandro Manzoni. They tell me that there are well organized cattle and dairy farms all over.

The local Church is well organized, serious, faithful to the rites, functions, charitable activities, and tradition. There aren't any important stimuli, and you don't hear the prophesy—sometimes a little transgressive—that you hear in the Church in other countries. It's like a mother trying to do the best for her children while they would rather leave the house to go look for something else to do. The priests are all well prepared, unlike other places I've lived. There is a decent clergy with whom sometimes I have to argue, but I don't expect to be heard. It's our Church, and we have to love it.

The most important point of reference for me, of course, is our House. Despite the many adjustments of time, it retains the central entryway around which they have built new buildings. My room has a window overlooking a courtyard that we call "San Michele" and from which I can see the Tabor church, with its roofs at different levels, depending on the height of the naves inside. When it snows and the roofs are covered with white, you can see the windows lighted from the inside. It looks like a Christmas scene, quiet and a little romantic. Sometimes in our

249

To the Ends of the Earth

House there's noise from the children, youngsters and people who go there. Sometimes there is silence. When you walk down the long corridors, you cannot help but think of Frances Cabrini and the first Mothers who lived here—their sacrifices, their dreams, their hard and fruitful work. Tradition says that the Sisters grew silkworms, spun the silk and then weaved it. They had a workshop which went on to become a factory of rich fabrics in Codogno. We know that they had a vegetable garden and an orchard that was producing for the needs of the large family—forty Sisters, two hundred orphans, a hundred boarders, and other such residents. They had a barn with cows for milk, a chicken coop, and possibly some other animals.

One can not help but remember what was written in the Memories of the House, that the first Sisters were so poor that when they sat at the table "some ate with a single fork and and others shared one spoon." And they tell of the great cold, countered only with some stoves and some hot water bottles. Many Sisters fell ill with tuberculosis. One cannot help but go to the bedroom where Mother Cabrini slept and see her desk, her chair, her armchair, her devotions—all the things connected to her deeds and her prayers, her life as a pilgrim of God. And you can not help but meet the gaze of the Holy Missionary Child that Mother Cabrini always prayed to, especially when, stuck in Codogno due to illness or an inability to move, she asked Him to "go where she could not go." It tells of the tradition that the Holy Child gave a sign: his silken shoes became worn out

Fifty Years of Religious Life

and, although the Sisters fixed them, they wore out again.

Then, outside, off in another courtyard, is the large Tabor church that Mother Cabrini wanted to build but was not able to. But the General Superior who came after her eventually had it built. The relic of the heart of St. Frances Cabrini is preserved there. People come to pray before her heart. It takes in the anguish of so many people oppressed by grief. It really makes an impression to see the hope that her heart can radiate.

Here in Codogno, in 2008, I celebrated fifty years of religious life. It seems like the end of an apparently long parable. Upon reflection, it seems so short. Because we missionaries do so much, and always in a hurry. I do not know why. Even now, when I cannot go out anymore, when I don't often travel, when I move with caution, I always have to do everything right away. The pace is different and becomes increasingly slow, but there is always urgency.

Here I am learning to deal with old age with patience because I realize that patience is a great virtue. It makes us practice another virtue: *gratitude*. Anything, however small, that we manage to do when we feel that our heart is tired, that our mind requires rest, that the little bottles always contain more pills: each of these things raises a hymn of thanksgiving to God. I'm trying to learn that humility, which once had a different connotation, that is, to cure ambition and pride, while today it is to recognize ourselves always more radically dependent on God. Yes, we turn to this or that doctor when we feel bad, but

251

then we realize that no one can heal our fragility. It's up to us, and we should accept it with dignity, knowing that God loves the weak to confound the strong, and now everything depends on Him. It has always been so, but who took notice? Now I'm learning of the fragility of everything, that human relationships fade easily, and I find that the only ones left are those which we hadn't noticed before—the ones based on absolute gratitude.

The events and the alterations of which I have been the object, due to changes in roles not clearly expressed, which often made me feel bad, have taught me to confront myself. To sift through my feelings good and less good, to transcend that which is marginal to focus more on what is more important. If we do not find ourselves in certain situations, we cannot understand who we are and how we are made. We must walk on the coals of our inconsistency to face our weaknesses without being afraid, because before God we are free to be as we are. But we must make the effort to not split ourselves in two to be different in front of others.

So, slowly, with personalized teaching, God makes us understand what is important in life and why we must always immerse ourselves in discussion. In other words, we must grow spiritually. When the loneliness of thought and feelings and even of life makes us fall into the temptation of victimization, we must be alert not to fall into the banality that ruins everything. Solidarity with those near to us is worth more than all traitorous rationality. One day a Sister told me: "I have to settle for what others decide for me, even though it would please me to do otherwise, because, for now, this is what the Lord asks of me."

Keep an irrepressible yearning alive for eternity, for those things that last forever. If you still get involved in so many things, it's to be active and responsible. Even if we prefer seemingly mundane things (like my passion for sport, for reading, for music, for action movies where the hero does things impossible to believe, to save someone or something from disaster), it is only because that part of ourselves that contains the great desires tries to play down the seriousness of life. It makes me enjoy whole-heartedly the victories of our athletes or football players, or the hero of a movie.

Writing the history of our congregation is like writing my own history, less heroic and less grandiose, but a story in which God has marked every stage of life without a lot of noise in a great frame of apparent banality. It's a life like many others, only that when it's God who's writing, it changes everything. The history of our missionary life put me in contact with errors that could have been avoided in hindsight. But I do understand the courage that hundreds of missionaries have been able to muster by being faithful to a common destiny, a fragile and daring courage motivated only by a faith that directs our whole existence, despite mistakes. Such has been my life.

Now the words of the Psalms have become my prayers most used. I repeat a thousand times: "O God, you are my God, in the dawn I seek you..." (Psalms 63, 1). Or "I love you, Lord, my strength, who trains my hands for battle and my fingers for war...." Or again: "The Lord is my light and my salvation; whom shall I fear?" I understand that the battle continues and sometimes becomes even more difficult. It does not matter how far the goal, you still reach it by struggling in a constant discernment, which helps us not lose sight of it.

Now, even though my first morning prayers are brief, when I wake up, I say, "Thank you." And even though those of the evening are brief, before going to sleep I say: "Thank you." To God, of course.

www.ingramcontent.com/pod-product-compliance
Lightning Source LLC
Chambersburg PA
CBHW030332230426
43661CB00032B/1382/J